The Doctrine Of Power; Rightly Dividing The Supernatural

Selasi Noamesi

Published by Selasi Noamesi, 2024.

The Doctrine Of Power; Rightly Dividing The Supernatural
Selasi Noamesi ©2024

While every precaution has been taken in the preparation of this book, the publisher assumes no responsibility for errors or omissions, or for damages resulting from the use of the information contained herein.

THE DOCTRINE OF POWER; RIGHTLY DIVIDING THE SUPERNATURAL

First edition. July 18, 2024.

Copyright © 2024 Selasi Noamesi.

ISBN: 979-8227527752

Written by Selasi Noamesi.

Table of Contents

Dedication

I dedicate this book to Ellin Thomas, my mother in the faith. Thank you for your unwavering love, guidance, and support since my Bible school days. Your presence has been a great source of encouragement to me in good and bad times. I'm grateful for your prayers, wisdom, and belief in me. This book is a testament to your impact on my life. May God continue to bless and use you mightily!

Chapter 1

Introduction to the exploration

Theologically, the doctrine of power refers to the biblical teaching on the source, nature, purpose, and use of power.

What Is Doctrine?

A doctrine is teachings or a set of beliefs that are accepted as true and authoritative within a religious tradition.

In the Christian faith, doctrine is based on the Bible and is intended to summarize and interpret the teachings of Scripture.

The Greek word for doctrine is "dogma". However, in the context of Christian theology, the Greek word "didache" is also used to refer to doctrine or teaching.

"Dogma" typically refers to a formal decree, ordinance, or doctrine, often in a more formal or official sense.

"Didache" on the other hand, emphasizes the teaching or instruction aspect, and can be translated as doctrine, teaching, or instruction.

In the New Testament, both words are used to refer to the teachings of Jesus Christ and the apostles. For example, "dogma" is used in Luke 2:1 and Acts 16:4 to refer to decrees or ordinances.

"Didache" is used in Matthew 7:28, Mark 1:22, and Acts 2:42 to refer to the teachings of Jesus and the apostles.

THE DOCTRINE OF POWER; RIGHTLY DIVIDING THE SUPERNATURAL

In Christian theology, the term "didache" is often used to refer to the doctrine or teaching of the church, while "dogma" may be used to refer to a specific, formal doctrine or creed.

What Is Power?

In the biblical context, power is often associated with authority, strength, and capability.

Theologically, power can be understood in various ways:

God's power (omnipotence) is God's ability to do all things that are consistent with His nature and will.

Human power is the ability or capacity of human beings to accomplish things or exert influence over others.

Spiritual power is the power of spirits that enables people to accomplish spiritual feats.

Jesus' doctrine of power and authority

Luke 4:31-36 demonstrates Jesus' doctrine is connected to His power and authority in several ways:

Doctrine with power: Verse 32 states, "And they were astonished at his doctrine: for his word was with power." Jesus' teaching was not just informative but also transformative, carrying divine authority and energy.

Authority over unclean spirits: In verses 33-35, Jesus encounters a man possessed by an unclean devil. He rebukes the spirit, and it obeys, demonstrating His authority over the spiritual realm.

Power over the devil: The devil recognizes Jesus as the Holy One of God (verse 34), acknowledging Jesus' divine authority and power over the forces of darkness.

Amazement and testimony: The people are amazed at Jesus' doctrine and authority, declaring, "What a word is this! For with authority and power, he commandeth the unclean spirits, and they come out" (verse 36). This shows the impact of Jesus' teaching and demonstrations of power.

Jesus' doctrine is not just about conveying information but also about demonstrating His divine authority and power. His teaching is accompanied by spiritual energy, and His words carry the weight of transformation and deliverance. This is a testament to His identity as the Holy One of God, the Messiah, the Son of God.

Key theological aspects of the doctrine of power include:

The source of power;

God is the ultimate source of all power (Psalm 62:11, Isaiah 40:26).

The idea that God is the source of all power emphasizes His sovereignty and omnipotence. It also shows the dependence of all creatures on Him for their existence and abilities.

Self-existence is a characteristic unique to God. If any creature possessed power independent of God, it would imply that they are self-existent, which would contradict the biblical teaching that God is the only self-existent Being (Isaiah 44:6, John 5:26).

THE DOCTRINE OF POWER; RIGHTLY DIVIDING THE SUPERNATURAL

We can take a look at Luke 10:17-19 "And the seventy returned again with joy, saying, Lord, even the devils are subject unto us through thy name. And he said unto them, I beheld Satan as lightning fall from heaven. Behold, I give unto you power to tread on serpents and scorpions, and over all the power of the enemy: and nothing shall by any means hurt you."

The reason the evil spirits were subject to the disciples in the name of Jesus is because their powers and abilities aren't strange to God. They're created by God but they rebelled. The reason Jesus has given them authority over all the powers of the enemy is because these powers are original from God but now being used outside the original intent. If they had a self-existent powers, they couldn't be subject to the authority of Christ.

The purpose of power;

Power is to be used for God's glory, the advancement of His kingdom, and the benefit of others (Matthew 28:18-20, Mark 10:42-45).

Matthew 28:18-20 reveals Jesus' commission to His disciples to "go and make disciples of all nations," demonstrating the use of power for the advancement of God's kingdom.

Mark 10:42-45 emphasizes the importance of using power to serve others, as Jesus taught that true greatness comes from being a servant.

By recognizing the purpose of power, we can ensure that our pursuit and use of power align with God's intentions.

The use of power;

Power is to be exercised in love, humility, and service to others (Matthew 20:25-28, 1 Corinthians 13:1-3).

The limitations of power;

Human power is limited, and the ability to accomplish things is dependent on God's sovereign will and enablement (Proverbs 19:21, Isaiah 40:29-31).

Other creatures like angels, also have limited powers.

Now, in the context of this book, the doctrine of power refers to the idea that power and authority are not ends in themselves, but are meant to be exercised in accordance with God's love and for the benefit of others.

In other words, power is not to be used for personal gain, control, or domination, but rather to serve, bless, and uplift others. This perspective on power is rooted in God's nature, who exercises His power in a way that is always loving, redemptive, and life-giving.

The doctrine of power, therefore, emphasizes that:

1. Power is a means, not an end.

2. Power is to be exercised in love.

3. Power is for the benefit of others.

This understanding of power is in contrast to the way power is often exercised in the world, in rebellion, where it is often used for personal gain, destruction, exploitation, or domination.

In the context of our discussion, the doctrine of power highlights the importance of using our abilities, resources, and influence in a way that aligns with God's love and promotes the well-being of others, according to the purpose of God.

Chapter 2

God, The Source Of All Power

"In the beginning God created the heaven and the earth" (Genesis 1:1).

"In the beginning God...". With these four words, the Bible introduces us to the Source of all life, power, and existence. God is the fountainhead of everything that is, was, and will be, just as revealed in Revelation 4:8 "And the four beasts had each of them six wings about him; and they were full of eyes within: and they rest not day and night, saying, Holy, holy, holy, Lord God Almighty, which was, and is, and is to come."

God's creative power and wisdom brought forth the universe, and His sustaining power holds it all together, as revealed in Isaiah 40:26 "Lift up your eyes on high, and behold who hath created these things, that bringeth out their host by number: he calleth them all by names by the greatness of his might, for that he is strong in power; not one faileth."

And also, Psalm 147:4-5 "He telleth the number of the stars; he calleth them all by their names. Great is our Lord, and of great power: his understanding is infinite."

God as the ultimate Source extends far beyond the physical realm. He is also the Source of all spiritual power, gifts, and abilities—regardless of whether they are used in rebellion against Him or in fulfillment of His purposes. This fundamental truth is the starting point for our exploration of the doctrine of power and the supernatural. By acknowledging God as the ultimate Source, we lay the foundation for understanding the proper use and application of spiritual power, and the incredible potential that lies within us as His children.

Jesus revealed that God is the source of all authority and power:

"Then saith Pilate unto him, Speakest thou not unto me? knowest thou not that I have power to crucify thee, and have power to release thee? Jesus answered, Thou couldest have no power at all against me, except it were given thee from above: therefore he that delivered me unto thee hath the greater sin" (John 19:10-11).

Paul also revealed in Romans 13:1-2 "Let every soul be subject unto the higher powers. For there is no power but of God: the powers that be are ordained of God. Whosoever therefore resisteth the power, resisteth the ordinance of God: and they that resist shall receive to themselves damnation."

As the ultimate Source, God's power is not limited by human boundaries or definitions. His power is not just a means for getting things done, but an extension of His very nature and character. It is a power that is inherently creative, redemptive, and transformative. When we acknowledge God as the Source of all power, we begin to understand that every spiritual gift, ability, and manifestation is a reflection of His wisdom, love, and grace.

THE DOCTRINE OF POWER; RIGHTLY DIVIDING THE SUPERNATURAL

In this sense, God's power is not just a resource to be tapped, but a relationship to be nurtured. As we explore the doctrine of power and the supernatural, we will discover how to align ourselves with God's intended purpose, and how to harness His power in a way that honors His character and advances His kingdom.

Seeing God as the Source of all power and authority, we explore Him as the:

Creator:

God created the universe and everything in it, demonstrating His power as the ultimate Creator.

God's power is most evident as the Creator of the universe and everything in it. The Bible says in Genesis 1:1, "In the beginning, God created the heavens and the earth."

God's creative power is awe-inspiring, and it's a testament to His wisdom, knowledge, and ability. He spoke, and the universe came into existence (Genesis 1:3). He formed the stars, planets, and galaxies with precision and purpose.

As the ultimate Creator, God's power is:

Omnipotent (all-powerful)

Omniscient (all-knowing)

Omnipresent (present everywhere)

God as the Creator demonstrates His sovereignty and majesty.

As Psalm 33:6-9 says, "By the word of the LORD were the heavens made; and all the host of them by the breath of his mouth. He gathereth the waters of the sea together as an heap: he layeth up the depth in storehouses. Let all the earth fear the LORD: let all the inhabitants of the world stand in awe of him. For he spake, and it was done; he commanded, and it stood fast."

Sustainer: He sustains all life, maintaining the delicate balance of nature and the universe.

Life-Giver: God is the source of all life, breathing life into creation and sustaining it.

Energy Source: He is the source of all energy, from the smallest subatomic particles to the vast expanse of the cosmos.

Spiritual Power: God is the source of all spiritual power, manifesting in gifts, talents, and abilities.

Authority: His power is the basis for all legitimate authority, whether in governance, leadership, or personal relationships.

Redemption: God's power redeems and restores, delivering from sin, darkness, and death.

Transformation: He transforms lives, communities, and societies, bringing renewal and restoration.

Wisdom: God's power is the source of all wisdom, guiding in truth, discernment, and understanding.

Love: His power is the essence of love, demonstrating selflessness, compassion, and grace.

Providence: God's power guides and directs, orchestrating circumstances for His purposes.

Miracles Source: He works miracles, defying natural laws and demonstrating His supernatural power.

THE DOCTRINE OF POWER; RIGHTLY DIVIDING THE SUPERNATURAL

Revelation: God reveals Himself and His plans through prophetic words, visions, and dreams, by which the Scriptures were written to be fulfilled in Christ the ultimate revelation of God.

Jesus is the head of all principalities and powers

As the Creator of the universe, Jesus has authority over all created things, including principalities and powers (Colossians 1:16).

Jesus is the sovereign ruler over all things, including spiritual authorities and powers (Matthew 28:18, Ephesians 1:21-22).

Through His death and resurrection, Jesus defeated sin, Satan, and all spiritual enemies, establishing His dominance over them (Colossians 2:15, Hebrews 2:14-15).

Jesus is the head of the Church, which is His body, and He has authority over all aspects of the Church, including spiritual powers and principalities (Ephesians 1:22-23, 5:23).

Jesus has all authority in heaven and on earth, and His authority is above all principalities and powers (Matthew 28:18, Ephesians 1:21-22).

In Colossians 2:10, Paul writes, "And ye are complete in Him, which is the head of all principality and power." This emphasizes Jesus' supreme authority and headship over all spiritual powers and principalities.

In Ephesians 1:21-22, Paul states that Jesus is "far above all principality, and power, and might, and dominion, and every name that is named, not only in this world, but also in that which is to come." This reveals Jesus' exalted position and authority above all spiritual powers and principalities.

Painting the supernatural picture of the conquest of Christ

THE DOCTRINE OF POWER; RIGHTLY DIVIDING THE SUPERNATURAL

The supernatural picture of Christ's conquest is a stark contrast to the futile attempts of human righteousness. Those who reject the righteousness of faith in Christ and seek to establish their own righteousness through works must undertake an impossible task. As Moses said, and Paul perfected in Romans 10, they must ascend to heaven and bring Christ down, then descend into the deep and bring Him up from the dead. In essence, they must replicate Christ's redemptive work by themselves!

This means they must:

Descend into the under regions, overcoming the powers of darkness and death;

Justify themselves in spirit, overcoming the accusations of the enemy;

Take the keys of death and hell by their own power;

Resurrect themselves by their own strength;

Ascend to heaven, overcoming the rebellious spirits in the heavenly regions;

Present themselves before God as perfectly righteous, satisfying all universal and eternal claims of justice.

This is the impossible standard of God's perfect righteousness. Anything less is not perfection before God. Yet, people still insist on trying to achieve it themselves, blinded by pride and ignorance of God's righteousness.

The righteousness of faith in Christ proclaims a different message: "You can't do it, but Jesus has done it for you! Believe in Him and be saved!" This is the word of faith that we preach, the word that is near us, in our mouth and in our heart.

As Paul wrote in Romans 10:8-10 "But what saith it? The word is nigh thee, even in thy mouth, and in thy heart: that is, the word of faith, which we preach; That if thou shalt confess with thy mouth the Lord Jesus, and shalt believe in thine heart that God hath raised him from the dead, thou shalt be saved. For with the heart man believeth unto righteousness; and with the mouth confession is made unto salvation."

Jesus has already conquered the powers of darkness, death, and hell. He has triumphed over all contrary powers and secured our salvation. As Colossians 2:14-15 declares, "Blotting out the handwriting of ordinances that was against us, which was contrary to us, and took it out of the way, nailing it to his cross; And having spoiled principalities and powers, he made a shew of them openly, triumphing over them in it."

Let us bask in the glory of Christ's supernatural conquest and rest in the finished work of our Savior!

Once again, Jesus is the head of all principalities and powers because of His creatorship, sovereignty, conquest, headship over the Church, and supreme authority.

Chapter 3

Power According To Relationship

We've seen that God's power is not just a tool to be used, but must be by intimacy with Him, a relationship to be cultivated. It's not just about accessing His abilities, but about deepening our connection with Him. When we view God's power as mere resource to be tapped, we risk reducing our relationship with Him to a transactional level. We may find ourselves only approaching Him when we need something, rather than pursuing a genuine intimacy.

When we recognize that God's power is a relationship to be nurtured, we begin to prioritize building a life-giving intimacy with Him. We invest time in prayer, study, and worship, not just to get something from Him, but to know Him more intimately. We learn to listen to His voice, abide in His presence, and to trust His guidance.

As we nurture this relationship, we discover that we don't only seek to encounter God's power but His Person. We experience His love, His grace, and His wisdom in ways that transform us from the inside out. We become like Him, representing and reflecting His character, extending His kingdom in the earth.

God's Original Intent Of Intimacy

God's original intent was to have a loving relationship with humanity. In the beginning, God created Adam and Eve to have a personal, intimate relationship with Him. He desired to share His love, wisdom, and joy with them, and to have them share their lives with Him.

In Genesis 1-2, we see God's desire for relationship with humanity, when He:

He created us in His own image (Gen 1:26-27)

He breathed His own breath into us (Gen 2:7)

He walked with Adam and Eve in the Garden (Gen 3:8)

He spoke with them directly (Gen 1:28-30; 2:16-17)

God's desire for relationship was not just about creating beings to worship Him, but about sharing His life and love with us. He wanted us to know Him, to trust Him, and to love Him with all our heart, soul, mind, and strength.

When sin entered the picture, God's desire for relationship didn't change. He pursued humanity, seeking to restore our relationship with Him through covenant, prophecy, and ultimately, through Jesus Christ.

Relationship over religion

Jesus Christ specifically said in John 14:6 - "...I am the way, the truth, and the life: no man cometh unto the Father, but by me."

He didn't say no man comes to heaven. God's purpose is first relationship with a Person before a place.

THE DOCTRINE OF POWER; RIGHTLY DIVIDING THE SUPERNATURAL

Every religion in this world believe in going to a heaven some day after death. Some religious groups even kill people in the name of getting better conditions in heaven someday; making a place the motive for worshipping a deity is idolatry and eternal hypocrisy, in wickedness.

Jesus brought a living relationship with the Father, this is greater than any place in a geographical heaven.

Jesus has said in John 17:3 - "And this is life eternal, that they might know thee the only true God, and Jesus Christ, whom thou hast sent."

Eternal life isn't primarily about going to heaven but knowing the true God in Jesus Christ who is the true revelation of the true God. The primal purpose of eternal life is intimacy with God in Christ.

Our predestination from eternity isn't to a place in heaven but to be conformed to the Stature of the Divine Person; it's said in Romans 8:29 - "For whom he did foreknow, he also did predestinate to be conformed to the image of his Son, that he might be the firstborn among many brethren."

We're predestined to the ultimate state of the Son of God, and not to a place in heaven. Our ultimate destination from "pre-destination" is beyond heaven, it's to the totality of the Son of God!

Will those possessing eternal life go to heaven one day? Yes. Should we be heavenly minded? Yes. But is heaven the ultimate purpose of eternal life? No. There's something eternally greater, beyond heaven; it's our eternal relationship and oneness with God in Christ.

Because of waiting to go to heaven, some people are living a religious manner of life without any living relationship with the Father in Christ.

Because of different doctrines of heaven there's hatred and segregation among brethren but true relationship with the Father is seen in love for the brethren.

Jesus dealt with some religious Jews without a living relationship, who claimed God is their Father, thus John 8:42 - "Jesus said unto them, If God were your Father, ye would love me: for I proceeded forth and came from God; neither came I of myself, but he sent me."

If we've a living relationship with the Father, we would love all the children of God!

Beloved, correct your ultimate motive and return to a living relationship with the Father in Christ.

Jesus Model Relationship

Jesus, the Son of God, was incredibly powerful when He walked the earth, yet He consistently demonstrated a deep relationship with His Father. He modeled for us what it means to prioritize intimacy with God, even in the midst of ministry and busyness.

In the Gospels, we see Jesus:

Often withdrawing to solitary places to pray (Luke 5:16).

Speaking with the Father in prayer, using intimate language like "Abba" (Mark 14:36).

Trusting in the Father's sovereignty and provision (Matthew 6:25-33).

THE DOCTRINE OF POWER; RIGHTLY DIVIDING THE SUPERNATURAL

Seeking guidance and wisdom from the Father (John 5:19-20).

Submitting to the Father's will, even in difficult circumstances (Matthew 26:39).

Jesus showed us that true power comes not just from self-ability or authority, but from a living relationship with the Father. He demonstrated that intimacy with God is the source of strength, wisdom, and guidance.

Jesus' intimacy with the Father was so deep that He could say:

"The words I say to you are not my own, but the Father's who sent me" (John 14:24): "For I have not spoken of myself; but the Father which sent me, he gave me a commandment, what I should say and what I should speak."

"By myself I can do nothing; I judge only as I hear, and my judgment is just, for I seek not to please myself but him who sent me" (John 5:30): "I can of mine own self do nothing: as I hear, I judge: and my judgment is just; because I seek not mine own will, but the will of the Father which hath sent me."

"The Father is always at work, and so am I" (John 5:17): "But Jesus answered them, My Father worketh hitherto, and I work."

"I can do nothing on my own initiative; I judge only as I hear, and my judgment is just, because I am not seeking my own will but the will of him who sent me" (John 5:30): "I can of mine own self do nothing: as I hear, I judge: and my judgment is just; because I seek not mine own will, but the will of the Father which hath sent me."

Chapter 4

God's Love Regulates His Power

God's love regulates His power, meaning that His love is the guiding force behind His actions and decisions. His power is always exercised in accordance with His loving nature.

In other words, God's love is the why behind His power. He doesn't use His power arbitrarily or selfishly, but always with the goal of loving and blessing others.

God's love is the foundation of His relationship with us, and it guides everything He does.

As the apostle John wrote, "God is love" (1 John 4:8). His love is not just a feeling or an emotion, but the very essence of His being.

So, let's remember that God's power is always regulated by His love. He is a loving Father who desires the best for us, and His power is always used to achieve that goal.

"For God hath not given us the spirit of fear; but of power, and of love, and of a sound mind. (2 Timothy 1:7)

In the beginning, as we've been seeing, God created man in His own image, that He might have a people of love and to whom He might show His great love. But the fall of man had man's heart turned away from God.

Yet, God's heart was still towards man, and He sent His only begotten Son, Jesus Christ, to die on the cross for man's sins, that we might receive the life of God and be partakers of His divine nature.

THE DOCTRINE OF POWER; RIGHTLY DIVIDING THE SUPERNATURAL

Apostle Paul reveals that Jesus gave Himself for us because He loved us: "I am crucified with Christ, nevertheless I live; yet not I, but Christ liveth in me, and the life which I now live in the flesh, I live by the faith of the Son of God, who loved me and gave Himself for me." (Galatians 2:20).

In the old testament, the children of Israel were commanded to love the Lord their God with all their heart, soul, and might; but they could not, for they did not have the divine life of God.

But now, through the finished work of Christ Jesus, we have received the Spirit of love, and we can love God effortlessly, without pain or sorrow. For the Word of God saith, "For this is the love of God, that we keep His commandments, and His commandments are not grievous." (1 John 5:3).

And let us not forget the example of the disciples, who, when they were not received in a village, desired to command fire to come down from heaven and consume them, even as Elias did. But the Lord rebuked them, saying, "Ye know not what manner of spirit ye are of. For the Son of man is not come to destroy men's lives, but to save them." (Luke 9:54-56).

They wanted to demonstrate power without love, patience, and compassion.

Some people may think that showing judgment, cursing, or destroying others is a demonstration of power, but that's not the way of Christ. He doesn't take pleasure in destruction or use it as a proof of His power.

In fact, Jesus taught us to love our enemies, bless those who curse us, and pray for those who persecute us (Matthew 5:44). He showed us that true power lies in forgiveness, mercy, and love.

Some people surround themselves with the art of cursing, boasting in destroying others, revealing their own weakness and lack of understanding of God's love.

Let's remember that our Christ is a God of love, mercy, and grace. He desires to save and redeem, not destroy.

The New Testament priesthood is focused on saving and redeeming, and not cursing and destroying. Jesus' teachings and example are clear: He came to save lives, not destroy them.

The wisdom of the New Testament priesthood is rooted in love, mercy, and grace. It's about empowering people to come out of their weaknesses and into the light of the glorious gospel of Christ. Cursing sinners to perish in hell is not only unloving but also counterproductive, as it works against God's will and empowers the devil.

Instead, we should be praying for sinners to be set free from the devil's grasp and come into the love and redemption of Christ. We should be leading people out of fear and into genuine love, reverence, and respect for God.

Let's conform to the blueprint of the Melchisedecan priesthood, which is rooted in love and service. We should be doers of the word, living out the teachings of Christ and demonstrating His love and grace to all.

Remember, the will of God is not to keep people obedient out of fear but to raise them up in genuine love and reverence. Let's choose to walk in the wisdom of the New Testament priesthood, which is saving to the uttermost!

THE DOCTRINE OF POWER; RIGHTLY DIVIDING THE SUPERNATURAL

Thus, Hebrews 7:22-25 "By so much was Jesus made a surety of a better testament. And they truly were many priests, because they were not suffered to continue by reason of death: But this man, because he continueth ever, hath an unchangeable priesthood. Wherefore he is able also to save them to the uttermost that come unto God by him, seeing he ever liveth to make intercession for them."

The man of God should not misuse the power entrusted to him by destroying his brethren or cursing them. As a son of God, we are called to care for one another and gather into Christ, not scatter.

The Master's words are clear: "It is not the will of your Father which is in heaven, that one of these little ones should perish." (Matthew 18:14) We should not misuse our authority or power to harm or destroy others.

Instead, we should remember that we are all sons and daughters of God, and we should treat each other with love, respect, and care. If someone tries to curse us or harm us, we can stand firm in our identity as children of God and declare, "I won't perish as a son of God!"

Let's remember that God does not kill His sons and daughters. He is a loving Father who desires to save and redeem, not destroy.

Walking in love is essential to seeing God's power fully manifested in our lives and in the world. When we use our power to destroy others, even if they've made mistakes, we're not walking in love.

Once again, the Lord's words are clear: "Suffer none of these little ones to perish." (Luke 17:2) We should be praying for those who have offended us, not cursing them. And yet, many preachers and believers have cursed their brethren in Christ, even when they've made mistakes.

If we're already using the small power God has given us to destroy others, what would happen if He gave us greater power? It's crucial that we learn to walk in absolute love if we want to be used mightily by God according to His purpose.

Winning souls into Christ and then cursing them when they offend us is eternal hypocrisy. We need to understand God's eternal purpose and recognize that we're all imperfect in ourselves, making mistakes and in need of grace, so we don't curse others when they offend us.

The Bible says in Ephesians 4:11-12, "And he gave some, apostles; and some, prophets; and some, evangelists; and some, pastors and teachers; For the perfecting of the saints, for the work of the ministry, for the edifying of the body of Christ."

The gifts of apostles, prophets, and other five-fold ministry gifts are given to edify (build up) the body of Christ, not to destroy.

Every believer, even when they offend us, is still a part of the body of Christ.

So, we correct them in love, praying for their change, in patience.

THE DOCTRINE OF POWER; RIGHTLY DIVIDING THE SUPERNATURAL

In 1 Corinthians 14:3-5, Paul writes, "But he that prophesieth speaketh unto men to edification, and exhortation, and comfort. He that speaketh in an unknown tongue edifieth himself; but he that prophesieth edifieth the church... I would that ye all spake with tongues, but rather that ye prophesied: for greater is he that prophesieth than he that speaketh with tongues, except he interpret, that the church may receive edifying."

The purpose of these gifts is to build up, encourage, and console the body of Christ, not to tear it down or destroy it. Let's use our gifts and abilities to edify and bless others, not to hurt or destroy them!

All Things Flow Out Of God's Love

All other things flow out of God's love. His love is the source, the foundation, and the motivation behind everything He does.

God's love flows into every aspect of His being and actions. His wisdom, grace, mercy, justice, and power all originate from His love.

In the same way, our relationship with God should also flow from His love. Love is the spirit of our manifestation; our trust, obedience, worship, and service should all be motivated by His love.

Jesus said to the disciples in John 14:15 "If ye love me, keep my commandments."

As the Bible says, "We love Him because He first loved us" (1 John 4:19). His love initiates and sustains our relationship with Him.

So, let's anchor ourselves in His love, and from that foundation, allow all other things to flow.

In 1 Corinthians 13:1-3, Paul writes:

"Though I speak with the tongues of men and of angels, and have not charity, I am become as sounding brass, or a tinkling cymbal. And though I have the gift of prophecy, and understand all mysteries, and all knowledge; and though I have all faith, so that I could remove mountains, and have not charity, I am nothing. And though I bestow all my goods to feed the poor, and though I give my body to be burned, and have not charity, it profiteth me nothing."

In this passage, Paul emphasizes that without love, all his actions, gifts, and sacrifices are futile. Love is the essential foundation for any meaningful expression of faith.

The word "charity" in the verse is translated from the Greek word "agape," which refers to unconditional, selfless love. Paul is stressing that without this kind of love, even the most impressive spiritual gifts and acts of service are worthless.

This reminder is just as relevant today, encouraging us to examine our motivations and ensure that our actions are rooted in genuine love of God through us to others.

Chapter 5

The genuine supernatural, which is rooted in God's love, is distinguished from the rebellious or counterfeit supernatural by the presence of love. The rebellious creatures, lacking love, may manifest power, but it is devoid of love and ultimately leads to destruction.

In contrast, when we operate in the genuine supernatural, empowered by God's love, we manifest power that is transformative, redemptive, and life-giving. Love is the distinguishing mark of our actions, and it is what makes our witness authentic and compelling.

As I said, the absence of love in the rebellious supernatural beings leads to destruction. This is because, without love, power is misused and exploited for selfish or harmful purposes. But when we surrender to God's love and allow it to guide us, His power flows through us in ways that bring life, hope, and restoration to others.

The devil, also known as Satan, is the embodiment of evil and rebellion against God. He is characterized by a complete lack of love, and his actions are driven by pride, selfishness, and a desire to harm and destroy others.

In contrast, God is love (1 John 4:8), and His actions are always motivated by love, even when He disciplines.

The Bible describes Satan as a "liar and the father of lies" (John 8:44), who "comes to steal, kill, and destroy" (John 10:10). His rebellion against God is rooted in his own pride and selfishness, and he seeks to draw others into his rebellion.

On the other hand, God's love is pure, selfless, and re-demptive, as revealed in Christ. He "is patient, love is kind" (1 Corinthians 13:4), and His "love endureth forever" (Psalm 136:1-3). God's love is the antidote to the devil's evil, and it is the source of our salvation and transformation.

By recognizing the difference between God's love and the devil's lack of love, we can better understand the spiritual forces at work in our lives and make choices that align with God's love and purposes.

Witches, for example, operate out of a desire for power, control, and self-interest, which stem from a lack of love and relationship with God.

James 3:13-18 says "Who is a wise man and endued with knowledge among you? let him shew out of a good conversation his works with meekness of wisdom. But if ye have bitter envying and strife in your hearts, glory not, and lie not against the truth. This wisdom descendeth not from above, but is earthly, sensual, devilish. For where envying and strife is, there is confusion and every evil work. But the wisdom that is from above is first pure, then peaceable, gentle, and easy to be in-treated, full of mercy and good fruits, without partiality, and without hypocrisy. And the fruit of righteousness is sown in peace of them that make peace."

When we walk in God's love, our actions are infused with kindness, compassion, and a desire to bless and serve others. This is the essence of God's kingdom, where love reigns supreme and power is used for the greater good.

Rebellious use of power

THE DOCTRINE OF POWER; RIGHTLY DIVIDING THE SUPERNATURAL

But what about when spiritual power is used in rebellion against God? How can we reconcile the fact that God is the Source of all power with the reality of spiritual abuse, manipulation, and control? The answer lies in understanding that even in rebellion, spiritual power is still what God had given a creature to be used according to His original purpose before the creature's rebellion. It is a perversion of original intent.

In this sense, the misuse of spiritual power is not a negation of God's sovereignty and authority, but a twisted affirmation of it. It is a testament to the fact that God's power is so great, so vast, and so available that even in rebellion, it can be tapped and exploited.

When a creature uses spiritual power in rebellion against God, it's both an abuse and misrepresentation of His character, suggesting that God is something He is not, that He is willing to compromise His own wisdom, love, and grace for a creature's own selfish ends.

And that's why it's so important for us to align ourselves with God's intended purpose, to harness His power in a way that honors His character and advances His kingdom. When we do, we become conduits of His grace, channels of His love, and manifestations of His wisdom.

The Never-Diminishing God

As we've seen that God is the ultimate source of all gifts and abilities, we understand that He has generously bestowed talents and skills on every creature, big or small; whether the creatures use these things in rebellion or not, it's still God's abilities being used in or out of purpose.

As a matter of truth, every gift and ability we possess is still present in God, in a perfect and supreme way.

If God gives you a gift or ability and He ceases to possess such in Himself, it would mean that He has to depend on you alone when it comes to the purpose of such ability in creation. It would mean that, if you rebel against God, you'll now possess an ability God doesn't possess so you can outwit Him in that area.

However, the above will never happen in any version of existence.

Every true and even corrupted gifts, talents and abilities still remain in Him, original and pure according to the original intent.

That's why you don't use corrupt gifts to limit Him, that because creatures of darkness operate the counterfeit, God is banned from operating the original.

When the Egyptian magicians thought they possessed the ability to do what Moses could do by God's power, God did show them something higher than their powers, and they confessed that Moses was working by the finger (spirit) of God!

This is the reality of God the source of all things!

He can give out of Himself and it's like nothing is gone out of Him, for His essence can't be diminished in any way.

Blessed be His fullness!

Chapter 6

THE COUNTERFEIT SUPERNATURAL

God is the creator of all things. There is nothing created that is not by Him.

John 1:3 says "All things were made by him; and without him was not any thing made that was made".

Colossians 1:16 also reiterated, "For by him were all things created, that are in heaven, and that are in earth, visible and invisible, whether they be thrones, or dominions, or principalities, or powers: all things were created by him, and for him:"

Everything that calls itself "gods" today were all created by God almighty but they rebelled with the devil.

The Bible says in Revelation 12:7 - "And there was war in heaven: Michael and his angels fought against the dragon; and the dragon fought and his angels,

8 And prevailed not; neither was their place found any more in heaven.

9 And the great dragon was cast out, that old serpent, called the Devil, and Satan, which deceiveth the whole world: he was cast out into the earth, and his angels were cast out with him".

This is when they rebelled and were cast out of heaven, and they came to establish their kingdom in the earth realm, deceiving men to worship them as gods.

What the devil did was to deceive many angels from different categories of the angelic race to join him in his rebellion.

That is why he has some of the angels from every category of the angelic rank in his kingdom.

Ephesians 6:12 says, "For we wrestle not against flesh and blood, but against principalities, against powers, against the rulers of the darkness of this world, against spiritual wickedness in high places".

These are fallen supernatural creatures who are now on the devil's side working against the Kingdom of God.

Even though the devil has some of these angels from various angelic ranks in his kingdom, there is the majority of angels from these same ranks which are still with God as holy angels.

We have principalities, thrones, dominions, powers and other angelic ranks still in God's kingdom.

It was when these angels fell that they now perverted that which God created for His good purpose.

Their powers and abilities had become evil, and they started to use such against God and His creation.

It is said of Lucifer, now the devil, in Ezekiel 28:17 - "Thine heart was lifted up because of thy beauty, thou hast corrupted thy wisdom by reason of thy brightness:.."

He corrupted his wisdom!

Evil is from the "d-evil".

The Lord Jesus said the devil is the murderer from the beginning.

There is the fallen angel of magic but that angel fell from a category of angels who are in charge of such abilities, just that the fallen one has now perverted his ability and has taught men to do such acts in a perverted way.

THE DOCTRINE OF POWER; RIGHTLY DIVIDING THE SUPERNATURAL

You can see that in the kingdom of darkness people could do divinations and consult familiar spirits, and prophesy accurately with such evil spirits, because they were created for such originally but when they fell perverted it.

Whatever we see in the kingdom of darkness is a perversion and adulteration of the true and right one in light.

This is why God challenged the gods of Egypt through Aaron and Moses.

2 "And the LORD said unto him, What is that in thine hand? And he said, A rod.

3 And he said, Cast it on the ground. And he cast it on the ground, and it became a serpent; and Moses fled from before it.

4 And the LORD said unto Moses, Put forth thine hand, and take it by the tail. And he put forth his hand, and caught it, and it became a rod in his hand:" (Exodus 4).

This is what the fallen angels of magic taught the magicians of Egypt but God has demonstrated to us that He is the source of all power, that those people may have perverted it but He is the true and right source of all powers.

8 "And the LORD spake unto Moses and unto Aaron, saying,

9 When Pharaoh shall speak unto you, saying, Shew a miracle for you: then thou shalt say unto Aaron, Take thy rod, and cast it before Pharaoh, and it shall become a serpent.

10 And Moses and Aaron went in unto Pharaoh, and they did so as the LORD had commanded: and Aaron cast down his rod before Pharaoh, and before his servants, and it became a serpent.

11 Then Pharaoh also called the wise men and the sorcerers: now the magicians of Egypt, they also did in like manner with their enchantments.

12 For they cast down every man his rod, and they became serpents: but Aaron's rod swallowed up their rods" (Exodus 7).

We can see that the true and right source of power would always overcome the counterfeit.

This principle is in John 1:5 that "And the light shineth in darkness; and the darkness comprehended it not".

The magicians could do what Aaron did but in a perverted way of enchantments which in this case worsened their plagues than solved them.

6 "And Aaron stretched out his hand over the waters of Egypt; and the frogs came up, and covered the land of Egypt.

7 And the magicians did so with their enchantments, and brought up frogs upon the land of Egypt.

8 Then Pharaoh called for Moses and Aaron, and said, Intreat the LORD, that he may take away the frogs from me, and from my people; and I will let the people go, that they may do sacrifice unto the LORD.

9 And Moses said unto Pharaoh, Glory over me: when shall I intreat for thee, and for thy servants, and for thy people, to destroy the frogs from thee and thy houses, that they may remain in the river only?

10 And he said, To morrow. And he said, Be it according to thy word: that thou mayest know that there is none like unto the LORD our God" (Exodus 8).

It was darkness that was now bowing to light.

THE DOCTRINE OF POWER; RIGHTLY DIVIDING THE SUPERNATURAL

This is what happened in Ephesus in the days of the early Apostles, when the true power of God was demonstrated so much that it is recorded in Acts 19:19 that "Many of them also which used curious arts brought their books together, and burned them before all men: and they counted the price of them, and found it fifty thousand pieces of silver".

It is the same thing we could see with Simon the sorcerer:

5 "Then Philip went down to the city of Samaria, and preached Christ unto them.

6 And the people with one accord gave heed unto those things which Philip spake, hearing and seeing the miracles which he did.

7 For unclean spirits, crying with loud voice, came out of many that were possessed with them: and many taken with palsies, and that were lame, were healed.

8 And there was great joy in that city.

9 But there was a certain man, called Simon, which beforetime in the same city used sorcery, and bewitched the people of Samaria, giving out that himself was some great one:

10 To whom they all gave heed, from the least to the greatest, saying, This man is the great power of God.

11 And to him they had regard, because that of long time he had bewitched them with sorceries.

12 But when they believed Philip preaching the things concerning the kingdom of God, and the name of Jesus Christ, they were baptized, both men and women.

13 Then Simon himself believed also: and when he was baptized, he continued with Philip, and wondered, beholding the miracles and signs which were done" (Acts 8).

Simon could see the greater power from the true and right source, and even opted to buy it later.

When the true and right source of power is demonstrated, the counterfeit shrinks away in shame!

16 "And it came to pass, as we went to prayer, a certain damsel possessed with a spirit of divination met us, which brought her masters much gain by soothsaying:

17 The same followed Paul and us, and cried, saying, These men are the servants of the most high God, which shew unto us the way of salvation.

18 And this did she many days. But Paul, being grieved, turned and said to the spirit, I command thee in the name of Jesus Christ to come out of her. And he came out the same hour" (Acts 16).

The spirit of divination could give accurate prophecies but when the true Spirit comes in authority the spirit of darkness has to bow!

God called these rebellious creatures which call themselves gods, an abomination.

Thus, Isaiah : 41 : 22 - "Let them bring them forth, and shew us what shall happen: let them shew the former things, what they be, that we may consider them, and know the latter end of them; or declare us things for to come.

23 Shew the things that are to come hereafter, that we may know that ye are gods: yea, do good, or do evil, that we may be dismayed, and behold it together.

24 Behold, ye are of nothing, and your work of nought: an abomination is he that chooseth you."

And again, 1 Kings 11:5 - "For Solomon went after Ashtoreth the goddess of the Zidonians, and after Milcom the abomination of the Ammonites."

God was just against such rebellious beings.

They could not stand God in the Old Testament as with the false god, Dagon.

1 "And the Philistines took the ark of God, and brought it from Ebenezer unto Ashdod.

2 When the Philistines took the ark of God, they brought it into the house of Dagon, and set it by Dagon.

3 And when they of Ashdod arose early on the morrow, behold, Dagon was fallen upon his face to the earth before the ark of the LORD. And they took Dagon, and set him in his place again.

4 And when they arose early on the morrow morning, behold, Dagon was fallen upon his face to the ground before the ark of the LORD; and the head of Dagon and both the palms of his hands were cut off upon the threshold; only the stump of Dagon was left to him.

5 Therefore neither the priests of Dagon, nor any that come into Dagon's house, tread on the threshold of Dagon in Ashdod unto this day.

6 But the hand of the LORD was heavy upon them of Ashdod, and he destroyed them, and smote them with emerods, even Ashdod and the coasts thereof.

7 And when the men of Ashdod saw that it was so, they said, The ark of the God of Israel shall not abide with us: for his hand is sore upon us, and upon Dagon our god.

8 They sent therefore and gathered all the lords of the Philistines unto them, and said, What shall we do with the ark of the God of Israel? And they answered, Let the ark of the God of Israel be carried about unto Gath. And they carried the ark of the God of Israel about thither.

9 And it was so, that, after they had carried it about, the hand of the LORD was against the city with a very great destruction: and he smote the men of the city, both small and great, and they had emerods in their secret parts.

10 Therefore they sent the ark of God to Ekron. And it came to pass, as the ark of God came to Ekron, that the Ekronites cried out, saying, They have brought about the ark of the God of Israel to us, to slay us and our people.

11 So they sent and gathered together all the lords of the Philistines, and said, Send away the ark of the God of Israel, and let it go again to his own place, that it slay us not, and our people: for there was a deadly destruction throughout all the city; the hand of God was very heavy there.

12 And the men that died not were smitten with the emerods: and the cry of the city went up to heaven" (1 Samuel 5).

They are all false gods!

The prophet Elijah also exposed the fake Baal, triumphing over it in the name of the Lord God of Israel.

The Demands of False Gods

Why did God choose Abraham and call him out of idol worship? Why did He entrust His true ways to him in types and shadows until the coming of Christ Jesus?

THE DOCTRINE OF POWER; RIGHTLY DIVIDING THE SUPERNATURAL

One reason God asked Abraham to sacrifice Isaac was to show that He is not like the false gods who demand human blood. God provided a substitute ram, demonstrating His power over life and death. God proved He's not bloodthirsty like the false gods by providing a substitute ram for Isaac. By staying Abraham's hand and providing a substitute, God showed that He is a God of mercy and redemption, not a consumer of human blood like the false gods.

This event foreshadowed the ultimate sacrifice of Christ Jesus, which was predetermined in God's plan.

It's important to note that sacrifice of bulls and goats was not part of God's original plan. He made this clear throughout the Bible, such as in:

1 Samuel 15:22-23 "And Samuel said, Hath the Lord as great delight in burnt offerings and sacrifices, as in obeying the voice of the Lord? Behold, to obey is better than sacrifice, and to hearken than the fat of rams. For rebellion is as the sin of witchcraft, and stubbornness is as iniquity and idolatry."

Psalm 40:6-8 "Sacrifice and offering thou didst not desire; mine ears hast thou opened: burnt offering and sin offering hast thou not required. Then said I, Lo, I come: in the volume of the book it is written of me, I delight to do thy will, O my God: yea, thy law is within my heart."

Hosea 6:6 "For I desired mercy, and not sacrifice; and the knowledge of God more than burnt offerings."

These passages emphasize God's desire for obedience and mercy over sacrifice.

In contrast, false gods even demand human sacrifice, which is diabolic. People offer humans to their gods, stools, and idols, some unaware that this is not to the Almighty God. God's original intent was for humans to obey Him, not to offer sacrifices.

The Bible also shows that God does not delight in bloodshed, as expressed in 1 Chronicles 22:7-8 "And David said to Solomon, My son, as for me, it was in my mind to build an house unto the name of the Lord my God: But the word of the Lord came to me, saying, Thou hast shed blood abundantly, and hast made great wars: thou shalt not build an house unto my name, because thou hast shed much blood upon the earth in my sight."

David was disqualified from building the temple because of his involvement in wars and bloodshed.

Now that Jesus has resurrected, there is no need for further animal sacrifice. God accepts no animal sacrifice or any other form of sacrifice. We can identify false gods by their demand for blood and know that they are not true.

God's original intent was for humans to obey Him, not to offer sacrifices. False gods demand human sacrifice, which is diabolic. The ultimate sacrifice of Christ Jesus was predetermined in God's plan, and now there is no need for further sacrifice.

If Adam had obeyed God and eaten from the Tree of Life, he would have been consummated in the life of Christ, which was symbolized in the Tree of Life. This would have meant that Adam would have been fully united with God, and would have experienced the fullness of divine life and fellowship with God.

THE DOCTRINE OF POWER; RIGHTLY DIVIDING THE SUPERNATURAL

In this sense, the Tree of Life represented the ultimate goal of human existence, which is to be fully united with God and to experience the fullness of His life and intimacy. By eating from the Tree of Life, Adam would have been able to participate in the divine nature and would have been transformed into the image of the risen Christ, who is the true Tree of Life.

The emphasis on Christ's sacrifice is His obedience, which undoes the disobedience of the first Adam and reconciles us to the life that Adam forfeited.

In Romans 5:19, Paul writes, "For as by one man's disobedience many were made sinners, so by the obedience of one shall many be made righteous." This reveals the contrast between Adam's disobedience and Christ's obedience.

Christ's obedience unto death on the cross (Philippians 2:8) reversed the effects of Adam's disobedience and restored our relationship with God. Through Christ's obedience, we are reconciled to the life that Adam forfeited, which is the life of union and fellowship with God.

This shows that Christ's sacrifice was not just about paying a penalty for sin, but also about demonstrating His obedience and undoing the effects of Adam's disobedience. By doing so, Christ restored our access to the Tree of Life, which symbolizes the fullness of divine life and fellowship with God.

So, the sacrifice of Christ was not because God was bloodthirsty, but because of His immense love for humanity. God's desire was to reconcile humanity to Himself, and Christ's sacrifice was the ultimate expression of that love.

By raising Christ from the dead, God demonstrated His power over life and death, and showed that He is not like the false gods who demand blood sacrifices but have no power to give life. This act of resurrection also shows God's mercy and His desire to save humanity, rather than demanding bloodshed.

In contrast to the false gods, the true God is a God of love, mercy, and redemption. He is not a consumer of human blood, but a giver of life and salvation. Through Christ's sacrifice and resurrection, God has shown us His true character and His desire to save humanity from the grip of sin, death, and the deception of the rebellious spirit beings.

Chapter 7

Telling the chaff to the wheat

"The prophet that hath a dream, let him tell a dream; and he that hath my word, let him speak my word faithfully. What is the chaff to the wheat? saith the Lord" (Jeremiah 23:28).

Both the natural life and the divine life is all about discerning the chaff to the wheat according to the principle in the above verse.

We don't destroy the wheat with the chaff because of the chaff but sieve, separate them by wisdom.

This is the same principle used by God Himself when man sinned and the genetic nature of sin was blended with him; God didn't destroy man utterly, in cessation of life in essential existence because of sin but by wisdom destroyed sin in Christ Jesus so as to save man eternally in the Risen Christ.

This principle is always used by God that's why He didn't destroy even the rebellious spirit beings but still left them till the consummation of His infinite wisdom.

We can see this principle literally from the parable the Master gave in Matthew 13:24 "Another parable put he forth unto them, saying, The kingdom of heaven is likened unto a man which sowed good seed in his field: [25] But while men slept, his enemy came and sowed tares among the wheat, and went his way. [26] But when the blade was sprung up, and brought forth fruit, then appeared the tares also. [27] So the servants of the householder came and said unto him, Sir, didst not thou sow good seed in thy field? from whence then hath it tares? [28] He said unto them, An enemy hath done this. The servants said unto him, Wilt thou then that we go and gather them up? [29] But he said, Nay; lest while ye gather up the tares, ye root up also the wheat with them. [30] Let both grow together until the harvest: and in the time of harvest I will say to the reapers, Gather ye together first the tares, and bind them in bundles to burn them: but gather the wheat into my barn."

This principle works in every area of existence.

There are fake politicians but we don't say politics should be destroyed because of the fake ones.

There are fake doctors, lawyers, there are wicked criminals in a nation but we don't destroy the whole nation because of the fake ones.

This principle also applies to spiritual things even in the Church and Kingdom of Christ Jesus; the fact that there are fake stuffs, doesn't mean the whole church, the whole Kingdom is concluded as fake, false and should be destroyed.

The fact that a spiritual gift is being abused or faked doesn't mean the genuine ones should also be destroyed or ignored altogether with the faked.

If that's the case then God Himself should be condemned and declared false and fake just because there are false gods all over in existence.

This is where maturity is in discerning according to all the factors in a particular case.

Some people don't want to grow in discerning things so they either accept all similar things as of the same source, and some also ignored all altogether with strong prejudice against any of such even of they're holy things.

However, life will always be by discerning.

THE DOCTRINE OF POWER; RIGHTLY DIVIDING THE SUPERNATURAL

We can see this principle again expressed in Hebrews 5:12 "For when for the time ye ought to be teachers, ye have need that one teach you again which be the first principles of the oracles of God; and are become such as have need of milk, and not of strong meat. [13] For every one that useth milk is unskilful in the word of righteousness: for he is a babe. [14] But strong meat belongeth to them that are of full age, even those who by reason of use have their senses exercised to discern both good and evil."

To be skillful in the word of righteousness isn't to condemn the wheat with the chaff just because of the chaff.

We'll keep discerning both good and evil in all things and ways.

We'll discern the realm of evil, and even when there's no evil anymore in existence, we'll keep discerning the realm of good and the realm of the holy.

That's to say, discerning isn't just between good and evil.

Even naturally, you choose between two good things at a time and let go of one not because the other is evil but because the chosen one is the one needed at the time.

It's said in 2 Timothy 2:15 "Study to shew thyself approved unto God, a workman that needeth not to be ashamed, rightly dividing the word of truth."

We're not only dividing the word of truth from falsehood in this case, but "the word of truth", that's to say, they're all truth by reason of the intent of God but we rightly divide all according to their right applications, positions, intent, purpose and implications.

We rightly divide them according to their ascent in God's original purpose.

To rightly divide in the above verse is likened to how a surgeon operates on a patient, cutting accurately without destroying other parts of the body, which implies that we don't let a realm of truth deny the existence of other realms of truth even if one is higher in purpose!

This is also expressed in Hebrews 4:12 "For the word of God is quick, and powerful, and sharper than any twoedged sword, piercing even to the dividing asunder of soul and spirit, and of the joints and marrow, and is a discerner of the thoughts and intents of the heart."

The fact that the soul is divided from the spirit doesn't mean the soul doesn't exist any longer.

The word rightly divides the joints from the marrow, and discerns the thoughts and intents of the heart.

The fact that there are evil spirits that have similar manifestations like the Holy Spirit doesn't mean similar manifestations of the Holy Spirit are evil.

God is the source of all gifts, operations and manifestations; the rebellious spirits just corrupt, pervert, abuse and use theirs out of original purpose and intent, thus independent of God the essential source.

A mature teacher of the word is one who rightly divides the word of truth, putting everything in their right places without destroying/condemning a particular truth as false just because of similarities, but just like the character of the word, he also pierces even to the dividing asunder of soul and spirit, and of the joints and marrow, and is a discerner of the thoughts and intents of all things by the word.

THE DOCTRINE OF POWER; RIGHTLY DIVIDING THE SUPERNATURAL

The fact that one isn't into "prophetism", healings, miracles, signs and wonders doesn't mean he should downplay them in his quest to establish his ministry and assignment.

People seem to have to always destroy other aspects of God's dealings in order to magnify their assignment or what they choose to major on while shutting themselves out of anything else God Himself would want to use them to do.

Sometimes in an attempt to teach people how to major on the understanding of the gospel even as they're going after healings, prophecies etc, some teachers tend to destroy the whole prophetic and healing ministries altogether, for instance.

But a mature teacher according to the wisdom of God can rightly divide these things without destroying others of God.

Every ministry is given by the wisdom of God and for vital purposes in the Church.

It's said in Ephesians 4:8 "Wherefore he saith, When he ascended up on high, he led captivity captive, and gave gifts unto men. [11] And he gave some, apostles; and some, prophets; and some, evangelists; and some, pastors and teachers; [12] For the perfecting of the saints, for the work of the ministry, for the edifying of the body of Christ: [13] Till we all come in the unity of the faith, and of the knowledge of the Son of God, unto a perfect man, unto the measure of the stature of the fulness of Christ: [14] That we henceforth be no more children, tossed to and fro, and carried about with every wind of doctrine, by the sleight of men, and cunning craftiness, whereby they lie in wait to deceive; [15] But speaking the truth in love, may grow up into him in all things, which is the head, even Christ: [16] From whom the whole body fitly joined together and compacted by that which every joint supplieth, according to the effectual working in the measure of every part, maketh increase of the body unto the edifying of itself in love."

The knowledge of the Son of God, the perfect man, the measure of the stature of the fullness of Christ is in all the gifts He's given as apostles, prophets, evangelists, pastors and teachers—they're all expressions of the Risen Christ, whether we like it or not.

To neglect and despise one is to be immature in the whole; it's possible that one be mature only in what he chooses to focus on, despising others, refusing to learn from them because to him he's knowledge of all things already, but that doesn't mean he's truly mature in all that God has given to the church in His wisdom.

We all have things to learn one from another through the lenses of the death, burial and resurrection of Jesus Christ.

For example, people say things like, just preach the gospel of "the death, burial and resurrection of Jesus Christ" and forget about any other manifestation of God in and through the church because they're not needed, they're useless and some even say such manifestations are of evil spirits, in the Church.

In as much as the centrality of the Gospel is the death, burial and resurrection of Jesus Christ, it's to an end and effect, and in the wisdom of God He's working out all things according to His purpose, even as we're still conforming to the image of the Firstborn Jesus Christ, vitally speaking.

THE DOCTRINE OF POWER; RIGHTLY DIVIDING THE SUPERNATURAL

After we've been born again, we establish people in the knowledge of Christ in all ramifications, thus to entrenched their understanding of their salvation, and we keep building them in all the other riches of His grace.

We've just seen in the verses above that we grow up into Him in all things, which is the head even Christ (all things are in Christ the head) and that every part of the body supply something essential for the rest of the body, thus, "speaking the truth in love, may grow up into him in all things, which is the head, even Christ: From whom the whole body fitly joined together and compacted by that which every joint supplieth, according to the effectual working in the measure of every part, maketh increase of the body unto the edifying of itself in love."

If we truly have the revelation of Christ, we would have this understanding as well.

People say, Christ is the complete revelation so nothing else is needed to be revealed in personal prophecies, healings and miracles among others, if that's the case then no one should teach another as well because Christ is in the born again already in the born-again believer, so Christ should express Himself in all ramifications with no one teaching anyone.

The reason you're teaching the born-again who already has Christ in him is the same reason God is working through others in various manifestations for corporate edification.

Chapter 8

Guided by Wisdom

One of the things that God taught me that's blessed my teaching ministry is how I don't destroy a biblical principle while establishing or teaching another.

Whenever I'm studying or teaching, I've all the principles in mind, so that I remain in the general biblical wisdom of God.

For example, Jesus Christ is called Prince, Michael is called Prince, the devil is called Prince, yet they're not the same, but used in different contexts, ranks and functions.

I shouldn't say because the devil is also called Prince, no one should call Jesus Prince.

"Man" for example, is generically used in the Bible; there are evil men, sinful men but Jesus is also called Man, with same original words yet Jesus isn't an evil or sinful man.

In fact, the Greek word "pneuma" is translated as human spirit, evil spirit, Holy Spirit, angels etc, yet we don't say ask people not to use it when it's translated as Holy Spirit because it's same word translated as evil spirit; we understand the source in context.

As a teacher or minister, I make sure I'm not carried away by "new insight/understanding/knowledge/revelation" to the extent of destroying other truths while talking about new insight.

Jesus for example, is called a lamb not because the lamb in the earth doesn't have negative traits, but because there's an aspect of the lamb that is analogously expressed.

THE DOCTRINE OF POWER; RIGHTLY DIVIDING THE SUPERNATURAL

The lamb is known to be unintelligent among others, yet Jesus is compared with its gentleness, and purity in sacrifice.

The same way Jesus is compared to lion because of boldness, and not because Jesus is devouring.

"The wicked flee when no man pursueth: but the righteous are bold as a lion" (Proverbs 28:1).

No matter the fallen trait of a creature, the original purpose and intent remains in God, so when used figuratively, in comparison with God or the believer, the negative side doesn't "define or redefine" God or the believer.

Our intellectual knowledge of the scriptures must be guided by the wisdom of the Spirit and spiritual things in Christ.

Don't be a double-standards preacher

In this world, if you want to use the devil as yardstick to judge the things of God, then you're not going to reside on the earth, you're not going to touch almost anything on the earth, and you're also not going to talk or speak dialects and languages.

Because everything has been corrupted, from a perspective.

Most words we use in languages and dialects were coined after satanic or corrupted perceptions. The names of days, months, etc, were coined after corrupt perceptions.

You'll be in bondage if you want to abstain from all these things in order to please God or be righteous and pure.

So, God Himself has revealed in Christ that all these things are His, and though they were corrupted, He's reconciled them in Christ.

The names may even remain unchanged but it's still in the principle of the spoil, where in ancient times, when a nation is defeated at war, for example, its belongings are taken as spoil, as sign of victory over that nation.

In this case, no creation in essence was the devil's in the first place.

So many words, phrases, and statements we use daily are etymologically rooted in corrupted perceptions, coined after rebellious creatures, etc.

This includes ideas and names of products we use everyday, even in the church.

However, we are not defiled by using these things because of the finished work of Christ. His redemption and authority allow us to engage these things without being bound by the corrupted understanding.

Some preachers who may not understand these things may be preaching double standards and using negativity as a yardstick to measure God's work; by trying to abstain from everything they deem corrupted in the world, they fall into legalism and bondage, instead of emphasizing God's grace, redemption, and the liberating power and authority of Christ, who reconciles all things to Himself, as the Creator of all things.

You would see some preaching such legalisms yet they're using words, phrases and statements with corrupted etymology. They're using platforms and products that are invented by unbelievers, and also being used for evil purposes.

If you want to abstain from one then abstain from all, and stop being a double-standards person, if not then understand the divine principle of how these things work in Christ.

THE DOCTRINE OF POWER; RIGHTLY DIVIDING THE SUPERNATURAL

I explore all creation through the lens of Christ

There's a mistake people make, when they try to teach the things of God through the lens of the devil, rebellion, or other religions. For example, someone claiming to be a former occult but now repent, is trying to teach the body of Christ through the lens of what they used to do in darkness. This will harm some believers than build them in the knowledge of Christ.

They tend to put people in bondage and independent of the wisdom of Christ, glorifying darkness.

Now, the wisdom of Christ is by the Holy Spirit alone in the Gospel and not people's experiences and practices in darkness.

Ephesians 1:17 says, "That the God of our Lord Jesus Christ, the Father of glory, may give unto you the spirit of wisdom and revelation in the knowledge of him:".

God's true spirit of revelation and wisdom in Christ is in the knowledge of Him (Christ) not through the lens of former occult experiences.

The same way, you don't teach against God's genuine gifts just because the devil copies or counterfeits them, saying things like "the kingdom of darkness also speaks mysterious languages so Christians shouldn't speak in tongues". It'll be contrary to the wisdom of Christ. You don't look at the devil to teach and explore Christ.

Christ is the Creator and Originator of all things, and darkness is only a corrupted version of God's original design. We shouldn't use the devil's counterfeit as a yardstick to measure God's genuine gifts. Instead, we should look to Christ, the Head of all Principalities and Powers!

"Don't Wear These Colors On These Days"

One of the demonic superstitions that put people in bondage is how some people go about telling others, including believers in Christ not to wear certain colors on specific days of the week, etc. It's very demonic, and undermines the universal authority of Christ Jesus, the victory of the believer, and his heirship in Christ.

The believer has authority over all things and colors. The believer is an heir of God, and joint-heir with Christ. Heirs are lords, having heavenly authority over all things in the earth, including all colors and all days...every color is made for man and not man for colors...that's to say, colors don't rule man, but man rules colors.

Mark 2:27-28 says "And he said unto them, The sabbath was made for man, and not man for the sabbath: Therefore the Son of man is Lord also of the sabbath."

This is a universal principle of man's authority. No day is greater than man. Man has authority over all days, and over all creation. The new creatures in Christ are lords over all things in existence, as joint-heirs with Christ.

Galatians 4:1 says, "Now I say, That the heir, as long as he is a child, differeth nothing from a servant, though he be lord of all;."

THE DOCTRINE OF POWER; RIGHTLY DIVIDING THE SUPERNATURAL

Those believers still observing colors for days, etc are servants to creatures instead of being lords over creation.

Verses 3-5 say "Even so we, when we were children, were in bondage under the elements of the world: But when the fulness of the time was come, God sent forth his Son, made of a woman, made under the law, To redeem them that were under the law, that we might receive the adoption of sons."

People are still in bondage to the elements of the world.

Verses 7-11 continue, "Wherefore thou art no more a servant, but a son; and if a son, then an heir of God through Christ. Howbeit then, when ye knew not God, ye did service unto them which by nature are no gods. But now, after that ye have known God, or rather are known of God, how turn ye again to the weak and beggarly elements, whereunto ye desire again to be in bondage? Ye observe days, and months, and times, and years. I am afraid of you, lest I have bestowed upon you labour in vain".

Sons (children) of God in Christ are lords over all. We don't observe and serve days, colors, and creatures! They serve us; we're not in bondage to them!

People may teach why you should do such but it's because they don't understand the truth of the finished work of Christ and the glory of God in His sons (heirs).

"Be careful on these days and months; they're named after these deities"

Some people teach the above statement, to exalt deities of Greco-Roman mythology above the universal authority of Christ by His finished work.

The fact that months of the year, and days of the week were named after certain "gods and deities" doesn't mean those deities are ruling those months and days.

We must understand that some of those things were done out of men's ignorance and misunderstanding. Some of these deities don't even exist. Even if they do, they aren't omnipresent to rule/operate everywhere.

A Christian who preaches and affirms that these deities rule months and days, clearly hasn't understood the revelation of Christ in His finished work, and the universal effect in every fabric of existence.

Those who preach, for example, that anyone who worships on Sunday is worshiping a sun god that Sunday was dedicated to, is clearly blaspheming, undermining the authority of Christ over all days. In fact, the person is attributing God's creation to another creature.

There's no day of the week that hasn't been dedicated to various deities by people around the world, so if we've to abstain from worshiping God Almighty on days because they're dedicated to deities then we'll have no day to worship He who created all days!

No deity created any day so stop attributing the glory of creation to them.

No one has the authority to declare any day a day of worship to their god and it'll have a universal effect on people worshiping the Almighty God on that day.

God alone is the Creator and Lord of all days.

People have free will, choice, faith, belief, and intent; God Almighty knows those who call upon Him (2 Timothy 2:19).

THE DOCTRINE OF POWER; RIGHTLY DIVIDING THE SUPERNATURAL

The purpose of the Gospel is also to reclaim God's creation that's ignorantly attributed to the devil and rebellious creatures—the purpose of reconciliation of all things to Christ.

This is what Paul demonstrated in Acts 17:22-24 "Then Paul stood in the midst of Mars' hill, and said, Ye men of Athens, I perceive that in all things ye are too superstitious. For as I passed by, and beheld your devotions, I found an altar with this inscription, TO THE UNKNOWN GOD. Whom therefore ye ignorantly worship, him declare I unto you. God that made the world and all things therein, seeing that he is Lord of heaven and earth, dwelleth not in temples made with hands;".

Once again, Christ has triumphed over all rebellious principalities and powers (Colossians 2:14-17), and everything in creation belongs to Him (Hebrews 1).

Christ has ultimate authority over all days and all worship.

He's the content and sum total of all things!

Even if the names of the days and months are still after gods and deities, it doesn't mean we're worshipping them by using such names, or operating in such months.

It's rather a sign of how Christ has made a public shew of them, spoiling them!

If Sunday was wrongfully dedicated to an imaginary sun god, I'll worship the Almighty Creator of all things, including the sun, on Sunday as proof of His Lordship on Sunday.

Chapter 9

Old tricks of the devil

The devil has studied the children of God in Christ, that to get them to stay away from anything that has great spiritual significance, he just has to be the first to manifest that and they'll label it devilish, though it's a neutral thing that anyone can use regardless of their religious affiliation or spiritual fraternity.

Some Christians used to be against (some are still against) speaking in tongues because they say it's Satanic. Some are against prophesying because people of darkness also prophesy/divine etc.

Some are against chanting in the Holy Ghost because to them it's only Eastern religions that chant. Some are against meditation in the Holy Ghost because they always hear dark religions say they're going to meditate or teach on meditation.

The devil knows this so he just has to be the first to use God's resources and the legal children would stay off as they are denied what is originally theirs.

The Master said by principle, in John 10:1 - "Verily, verily, I say unto you, He that entereth not by the door into the sheepfold, but climbeth up some other way, the same is a thief and a robber."

The devil isn't an originator but a thief, amazingly he steals that which is God's and the legal children of God stay off hence being robbed of what's theirs!

THE DOCTRINE OF POWER; RIGHTLY DIVIDING THE SUPERNATURAL

Whatever you see the devil manifesting or using or occupying, you should discern its original purpose and intent. Know his devices. Many fetish priests, magicians, demon possessed people, etc, were originally predestined to be great in Christ, the place for legal and right fulfilment of all purposes but the devil stole them for himself. The mad man of Gadara, the Mary possessed with demons, etc were all great but held down by the devil.

When Jesus delivered them, they indeed became great in light.

Don't let the devil trick you with this cheap device!

How The fear of the devil enslave their conscience in worry and fear

Some people are always worried about the devil, symbols, signs, etc; they're always trying not to do a sign that's attributed to the devil.

These people may not be spiritually mature in the knowledge of Christ and the mystery of the foolishness of the devil.

In essence, this world isn't for Satan but for Christ legally. Everything the devil might be doing to destroy the counsel of God is destined to fail.

Some people can't live peacefully in Christ just because of devil-consciousness.

People come out with many signs and symbols that they're for the devil to the extent that they can't freely express members/parts of their bodies without worrying if they've done a satanic sign etc.

Now people want to avoid rainbow colors just because a particular community uses it to represent their movement.

That's a defeatist mindset.

Nothing belongs to the devil.

He may just perverting the ones he wants but that doesn't mean the whole thing is devilish or satanic in its essence, concept and usage.

There are human beings that are possessed by demons by will but you don't call yourself demon possessed just because of them. If you're calling God's creature evil just because the devil copies and perverts its original intent, then you must declare yourself to be the same evil you see in every human being as well.

When Christians display their symbols and tokens like the cross, chapels, Bible etc, when unbelievers or satanist see them or watch them do they automatically get converted into Christianity? If no then why do you think just seeing satanic symbols and signs make you satanic?

Why are we restless in our legal territory?

When satanists watch our prayer meetings and church services do they get converted automatically?

Satan has no power to convert you automatically with symbols. That would make him greater and stronger than God who doesn't save people automatically by mere symbols.

When Satan came among the sons of God in the book of Job did it make the sons of God satanic automatically? Or did it corrupt God Himself?

Luke 4:5 says, "And the devil, taking him up into an high mountain, shewed unto him all the kingdoms of the world in a moment of time."

THE DOCTRINE OF POWER; RIGHTLY DIVIDING THE SUPERNATURAL

When the devil interacted with Jesus, whatsoever manner it may be, did it make Him devilish automatically or did Jesus also make the devil holy automatically?

The wisdom of Satan is what the princes of this world have and the word of God says it comes to nought, failing eternally.

They may have immediate results in the present evil world but fails eternally!

People of God, let's grow in the knowledge of Christ, living a life of peace of mind and of heart; don't be a son of God enslaved by devilish gimmicks that comes to nought.

Redemption Reappropriation

So, we've been emphasizing on Christ as the Creator and Originator of all things, who's come to reconcile all that went out of purpose or were being used out of purpose, back to the original intent.

We've understood that all ideas, concepts and misappropriation, were originally meant to reveal Christ.

God's original design and intent were always meant to point to His glory and love, as revealed in Christ.

Thus, by emphasis, Christ, the ultimate Redeemer, reappropriates by redemption, all things, including words, concepts, and ideas, to reveal His original glory.

For example, Paul's sermon in Athens (Acts 17:16-34) is a masterful example of reappropriation. He observed the Athenians' idolatrous practices and their altar dedicated to "the unknown god" (Agnotos Theos). He leveraged their curiosity and desire for knowledge to introduce them to the true God, Creator of the universe, which is Jesus Christ.

By quoting their own poets (Acts 17:28) and using their own concepts (unknown god), Paul reappropriated their language and ideas to reveal Christ, the ultimate truth. He showed how their own search for meaning and connection with "the unknown god" was ultimately fulfilled in Jesus Christ.

In many instances, the New Testament writers used words that had negative connotations in Ancient Greek, to mean positive things in Christ.

The Greek word "eirene", for example, which was associated with the Greek goddess of peace, "Eirene", is now reappropriated to convey the idea of spiritual, eternal peace, harmony, in reconciliation with God.

The same applies to the Greek word, "charis", which carried negative connotation in ancient Greek culture, associated with charm, allure, or seduction, often in a deceptive or manipulative sense. For example, the Greek mythological figure of Circe used her "charis" to lure and deceive Odysseus' men.

However, when Paul and other New Testament writers used "charis" to describe God's favor, grace, or unmerited kindness, they radically transformed its meaning, infusing it with a new, positive significance, according to God's original intent in Christ.

This redemption and reappropriation of language reveals how exhaustive the authority of God's redemption is in Christ.

Even the English word, "God", has negative connotations etymologically, but we use it for the Most High Creator today, and there's nothing wrong with it.

THE DOCTRINE OF POWER; RIGHTLY DIVIDING THE SUPERNATURAL

When Jesus says He is the Alpha and Omega, which is the Aleph and the Tav in the original Hebrew, (Revelation 22:13), He is declaring Himself the beginning and the end, the first and the last letters of the Greek alphabet, and the Hebrew Aleph-bet.

This metaphorically represents His role as the Creator and Redeemer of all things, encompassing the entirety of existence.

In essence, Jesus is the Author and Perfecter of language, meaning, and communication. All letters, words, and concepts, whether misappropriated or not, find their true purpose and meaning in Him.

By reappropriating language and ideas, Jesus redeems human understanding, restoring it to its original intent and purpose. He is the ultimate Redeemer, reclaiming and redefining all things, including language, to reveal His original glory.

What Did Jesus mean?

Considering Matthew 12:38-40, Jesus wasn't saying anyone who explores or walks in Holy Spirit signs and wonders is evil and adulterous.

Thus, "Then certain of the scribes and of the Pharisees answered, saying, Master, we would see a sign from thee. But he answered and said unto them, An evil and adulterous generation seeketh after a sign; and there shall no sign be given to it, but the sign of the prophet Jonas: For as Jonas was three days and three nights in the whale's belly; so shall the Son of man be three days and three nights in the heart of the earth."

Some people have misunderstood this, raising people in prejudice, to attack ministers who walk in genuine miracles, signs and wonders.

In the context of the discourse, the scribes and Pharisees, who were tempting Jesus, trying to trap Him in various ways, had already recognized Him as the Messiah but denied Him.

When one of the Pharisees, Nicodemus came to Jesus, he said "...Rabbi, we know that thou art a teacher come from God: for no man can do these miracles that thou doest, except God be with him." (John 3).

He said they, the Pharisees and leaders, knew Jesus is from God, but some denied it.

He acknowledging the miracles of Jesus shows the Pharisees had already seen enough to believe but they denied Him.

This kind of scribes and Pharisees, and the equivalent of unbelievers, who rejected Jesus Christ as the Messiah are the "evil and adulterous generation" He's referring to, and not those born again in Christ.

He said the sign these people would be given is the sign of Jonah, which speaks of His death and resurrection. The believer has already believed in the resurrection of Christ, and he's not tempting Jesus with hardened heart, so he's not "evil and adulterous" when exploring the glorious effects and manifestation of His resurrection power in miracles, signs and wonders!

THE DOCTRINE OF POWER; RIGHTLY DIVIDING THE SUPERNATURAL

True Signs and Wonders Versus Lying Signs and Wonders

Some people try to equate the works of the power of God in Christ to that of unbelievers in various religious groups and spirituality.

They would say, "miracles, for example, isn't exclusive to Christianity."

This is true but there's an eternal difference.

The power of resurrection is exclusive to those born again in Christ.

The Power of God in Christ is the power of the truth; it's of the resurrection of Christ in His finished work. It's manifestation is a testament to what He's accomplished.

It's the power of eternal life.

Apostle Paul by the Spirit said in Romans 1:16 "For I am not ashamed of the gospel of Christ: for it is the power of God unto salvation to every one that believeth; to the Jew first, and also to the Greek."

The Greek word for power in this particular verse is "dunamis" which is the same word for miraculous power or miracle working power or miracle itself.

So every manifestation of power in Christ, in the Holy Spirit springs from the same power that saves, even the resurrection power.

We don't have to lightly esteem it, deeming it common as the rebellious power in unbelievers.

The power at work in the rebellious world and spirits is God's power that's been perverted.

They still yield results but unable to save eternally; they're temporary, and fading away in relation to God's eternal purpose.

This is why their manifestation is called deceptive signs and lying wonders; it's because they don't issue from the power of eternal salvation; they can't save eternally.

God has authored a new thing called the resurrection power, which is a revelation none of the rebellious beings had.

The resurrection power is far above even the power that's at work in the holy angels, let alone the rebellious ones.

It's said in 2 Thessalonians 2:8 "And then shall that Wicked be revealed, whom the Lord shall consume with the spirit of his mouth, and shall destroy with the brightness of his coming: [9] Even him, whose coming is after the working of Satan with all power and signs and lying wonders, [10] And with all deceivableness of unrighteousness in them that perish; because they received not the love of the truth, that they might be saved."

That wicked is after the working of Satan with all his rebellious power, and signs and lying wonders but it can't save those who follow it and reject the resurrection power of Christ, which is "the love of the truth".

Many times people try to equate and compare pagan power to and with the power of God in Christ but they're not equal and the same; the death, burial and resurrection of Christ is the dividing line!

Just as we don't count the blood of Jesus Christ a common thing just because many people were also crucified on cross, but we know His crucifixion was special because of its purpose, we don't count anything that issues out of the work of the blood a common thing!

THE DOCTRINE OF POWER; RIGHTLY DIVIDING THE SUPERNATURAL

We revere and put premium on it; we glorify God for "the least" manifestation, because it's the sign and foretaste of the fullness to come, when all things are experientially consummated.

Chapter 10

The Purpose and Intent of Miracles, Signs and Wonders in this dispensation

Miracles, signs and wonders will not cease in this dispensation no matter how people oppose them, try to do without them, preach against them or trivialize them.

No one can outgrow miracles, signs and wonders in knowledge, that's to say, no one can come to a place where he'll say he know too much to be in need of miracles, signs and wonders. That'll only means the person is yet to know the purpose of these things.

Besides, the more one truly grows in the knowledge of God in Christ, the more the person grows in grace and peace.

The Apostle Peter captures this in 2 Peter 1:2 "Grace and peace be multiplied unto you through the knowledge of God, and of Jesus our Lord,".

And again in 2 Peter 3:18 "But grow in grace, and in the knowledge of our Lord and Saviour Jesus Christ. To him be glory both now and for ever. Amen."

Growing in the knowledge of God in Christ is growing in grace; it's the multiplication of grace and peace.

This is because the Lord Jesus Christ Himself is the embodiment of grace so you can't be growing in His knowledge and not be increasing in grace.

Grace here isn't talking about just the message that we've been saved by grace through faith, but also talking about every other gift, ability and power of God by reason of the finished work of Christ Jesus.

THE DOCTRINE OF POWER; RIGHTLY DIVIDING THE SUPERNATURAL

Peace has been under emphasized as well.

Grace and peace walk together; grace is consummated in peace.

We're saved by grace through faith, wherein we've peace with God!

Thus, Romans 5:1 "Therefore being justified by faith, we have peace with God through our Lord Jesus Christ:".

"Grace and peace" speak of eternal harmony between God and man; eternal harmony with all creation.

Jesus was full of grace and truth, then He rebuked the boisterous wind on the sea unto divine harmony, peace!

Thus, Mark 4:38 "And he was in the hinder part of the ship, asleep on a pillow: and they awake him, and say unto him, Master, carest thou not that we perish? [39] And he arose, and rebuked the wind, and said unto the sea, Peace, be still. And the wind ceased, and there was a great calm. [40] And he said unto them, Why are ye so fearful? how is it that ye have no faith?"

We can see the words, "faith", "perish", "wind", "peace", and the Master who's full of grace in the above verses.

By implication, wherever, people are perishing, whether eternally or bodily, "grace and peace" is needed there for God's original harmony. The Greek word for "peace" as used by Jesus in rebuking the boisterous wind speaks of silence, yet it's still the concept of harmony in creation.

"Grace and peace" is the full manifestation of the counsel of God in all creation.

Peace in itself is completeness, wholeness, prosperity etc.

Just like the Master, full of grace and truth, restored peace, perfect harmony within His disciples, the elements of air and water, in that scene, miracles, signs and wonders can't stop happening with the church, and sons of "grace and peace".

After talking about believing and confessing Jesus as Lord unto salvation, the Apostle Paul by the Spirit said bringing that message to unbelievers is bringing the gospel of peace.

Thus, Romans 10:15 "And how shall they preach, except they be sent? as it is written, How beautiful are the feet of them that preach the gospel of peace, and bring glad tidings of good things!".

Everyone preaching the gospel of grace is also preaching the gospel of peace.

"Grace and peace" is the gospel of the Kingdom.

The gospel of peace is the gospel of authority, power and dominion.

It's said in Ephesians 6:15 "And your feet shod with the preparation of the gospel of peace;".

Feet biblically stand for dominion, and the same time peace is also the consummation of God's dominion in the finished works of Christ Jesus, as linked to Romans 16:20 "And the God of peace shall bruise Satan under your feet shortly. The grace of our Lord Jesus Christ be with you. Amen."

The God of peace bruises Satan underneath the feet that's shod with the preparation of the gospel of peace.

This is the picture of dominion and authority.

THE DOCTRINE OF POWER; RIGHTLY DIVIDING THE SUPERNATURAL

So as we're saved by grace through faith, wherein we've peace with God, the harmony is extended to every other area of our living here on earth and in all eternities. This means that miracles, signs and wonders aren't only on human bodies but throughout all creatures.

"Let not then your good be evil spoken of:

For the kingdom of God is not meat and drink; but righteousness, and peace, and joy in the Holy Ghost" (Romans 14:17-18).

By this principle, anywhere there's evil, there's an opportunity for the manifestation of the Kingdom. Anything contrary to righteousness, peace and joy in the Holy Spirit, through the lenses of the finished work of Christ, is a prey for the Kingdom.

Jesus said in Luke 11:20 "But if I with the finger of God cast out devils, no doubt the kingdom of God is come upon you."

The finger of God is also the Holy Spirit, so even casting out devils is the manifestation of the Kingdom of God.

Just like casting out devils, every other miracles, signs and wonders are the manifestation of the Kingdom of God.

The Kingdom of God manifests miracles, signs and wonders now, and will keep manifesting them in all eternities so far as God is God and will keep revealing higher, unknown, unseen and untapped dimensions of Himself to His creation.

Even in the consummation of our eternal perfection, when no one will be sick or poor, signs and wonders shall still be there in diverse fashion, because every miracle, sign and wonder is revealing and pointing out something in God.

For example, after Jesus turned water into wine, it's said in John 2:11 "This beginning of miracles did Jesus in Cana of Galilee, and manifested forth his glory; and his disciples believed on him."

The Greek word for "miracles" in this verse is rather translated as "signs".

The turning of water into wine implies many things because it's a sign pointing to something in God.

You can't get to the things it implies if the sign wasn't shown.

In this instance His disciples believed in Him; even in the ages where all believe in God, His signs will trigger continous admiration and reverential worship.

In another instance, Jesus multiplied bread and fish to set the stage to introduce the people to the fact that He is the meat that endures unto eternal life; that He's the bread of life that has come down from heaven for life and immortality.

Thus, John 6:26 "Jesus answered them and said, Verily, verily, I say unto you, Ye seek me, not because ye saw the miracles, but because ye did eat of the loaves, and were filled. [27] Labour not for the meat which perisheth, but for that meat which endureth unto everlasting life, which the Son of man shall give unto you: for him hath God the Father sealed. [28] Then said they unto him, What shall we do, that we might work the works of God? [29] Jesus answered and said unto them, This is the work of God, that ye believe on him whom he hath sent. [30] They said therefore unto him, What sign shewest thou then, that we may see, and believe thee? what dost thou work? [31] Our fathers did eat manna in the desert; as it is written, He gave them bread from heaven to eat. [32]

Then Jesus said unto them, Verily, verily, I say unto you, Moses gave you not that bread from heaven; but my Father giveth you the true bread from heaven. [33] For the bread of God is he which cometh down from heaven, and giveth life unto the world."

You can't get to this message if He hasn't performed that miracle.

In God's infinite wisdom, He also confirms the Gospel of grace and peace with miracles, signs and wonders, just like He performed them to communicate divine truths.

This will continue throughout all eternity even in infinite perfection; we'll keep knowing God through signs and wonders as well.

It's said in Mark 16:19 "So then after the Lord had spoken unto them, he was received up into heaven, and sat on the right hand of God. [20] And they went forth, and preached every where, the Lord working with them, and confirming the word with signs following. Amen."

There are people who seem to be wiser than God Himself who's confirming the gospel, so they look down on what the Lord Himself is doing with other ministers.

Even if the minister isn't preaching the gospel accurately but miracles, signs and wonders are happening, they're meant to be interpreted through the lenses of the accurate Gospel and not to be rubbished.

In other words, the Lord is doing His part of confirmation of the already finished work of Christ Jesus but that minister is failing to do his part of preaching the accurate Gospel.

We saw something amazing in the dialogue between Nicodemus and the Lord Jesus.

Thus, John 3:1 "There was a man of the Pharisees, named Nicodemus, a ruler of the Jews: [2] The same came to Jesus by night, and said unto him, Rabbi, we know that thou art a teacher come from God: for no man can do these miracles that thou doest, except God be with him."

Miracles, signs and wonders follow every true teacher of the word, except they themselves shut themselves by prejudice.

We can also see in the discourse that God can't be with you and His signs won't be seen on you.

God is with all His children in Christ so miracles, signs and wonders will follow them.

Amazingly, Jesus related His miracles with being born again, seeing the Kingdom, being born of the Spirit as spirit.

Nicodemus was talking about Jesus coming from God, God being with Him, and so the miracles, then Jesus' answer was about being born again into the Kingdom.

Thus, John 3:3 "Jesus answered and said unto him, Verily, verily, I say unto thee, Except a man be born again, he cannot see the kingdom of God. [5] Jesus answered, Verily, verily, I say unto thee, Except a man be born of water and of the Spirit, he cannot enter into the kingdom of God. [6] That which is born of the flesh is flesh; and that which is born of the Spirit is spirit. [7] Marvel not that I said unto thee, Ye must be born again. [8] The wind bloweth where it listeth, and thou hearest the sound thereof, but canst not tell whence it cometh, and whither it goeth: so is every one that is born of the Spirit."

This implies that everyone that's born again, is come from God, God is with Him, and therefore can also do those miracles that Jesus was doing.

Seeing the Kingdom also speaks of the leading and manifestation of the Holy Spirit in the children of God.

The children of the Kingdom are children of signs and wonders, so Isaiah quoted Jesus, which is reiterated in Hebrews 2:13 "And again, I will put my trust in him. And again, Behold I and the children which God hath given me." As from Isaiah 8:18 "Behold, I and the children whom the Lord hath given me are for signs and for wonders in Israel from the Lord of hosts, which dwelleth in mount Zion."

We're the children given to the Lord Jesus Christ, as He said in John 17:9 "I pray for them: I pray not for the world, but for them which thou hast given me; for they are thine. [10] And all mine are thine, and thine are mine; and I am glorified in them. [11] And now I am no more in the world, but these are in the world, and I come to thee. Holy Father, keep through thine own name those whom thou hast given me, that they may be one, as we are."

Being one with God in glory above, you're for signs and wonders!

Since we've seen that every sign and wonder implies something in God and in His counsel, even all the signs shown by Moses in Egypt were communicating some things; which were in opposition to the acts of the Egyptian gods.

Not just with Moses but all the other signs shown in the Old Testament.

For example, it's said in 1 Samuel 5:2 "When the Philistines took the ark of God, they brought it into the house of Dagon, and set it by Dagon. [3] And when they of Ashdod arose early on the morrow, behold, Dagon was fallen upon his face to the earth before the ark of the Lord. And they took Dagon, and set him in his place again. [4] And when they arose early on the morrow morning, behold, Dagon was fallen upon his face to the ground before the ark of the Lord ; and the head of Dagon and both the palms of his hands were cut off upon the threshold; only the stump of Dagon was left to him."

The above sign was a prophetic foreshadowing of how the Lord Jesus Christ would spoil the devil and his cohorts, disarming them, triumphing over them in it.

Also, the miracles, signs and wonders of dividing the red sea, the pillars of cloud and fire, the manna etc were all signs with meanings in God, as the Apostle by the Spirit said in 1 Corinthians 10:1 "Moreover, brethren, I would not that ye should be ignorant, how that all our fathers were under the cloud, and all passed through the sea; [2] And were all baptized unto Moses in the cloud and in the sea; [3] And did all eat the same spiritual meat; [4] And did all drink the same spiritual drink: for they drank of that spiritual Rock that followed them: and that Rock was Christ."

It continues like this; Jesus multiplied food and said He's the bread of life; He opened the eyes of the blind and said He's the light of the world; He raised the dead and said He's the resurrection and the life, etc.

THE DOCTRINE OF POWER; RIGHTLY DIVIDING THE SUPERNATURAL

There were some signs that the Israelites and John the Baptist were supposed to see in identifying the Messiah, some of which are miracles, signs and wonders, as recorded in Luke 7:20 "When the men were come unto him, they said, John Baptist hath sent us unto thee, saying, Art thou he that should come? or look we for another? [21] And in that same hour he cured many of their infirmities and plagues, and of evil spirits; and unto many that were blind he gave sight. [22] Then Jesus answering said unto them, Go your way, and tell John what things ye have seen and heard; how that the blind see, the lame walk, the lepers are cleansed, the deaf hear, the dead are raised, to the poor the gospel is preached."

These were signs pointing to the Messiah, so it's also reiterated in Acts 2:22 "Ye men of Israel, hear these words; Jesus of Nazareth, a man approved of God among you by miracles and wonders and signs, which God did by him in the midst of you, as ye yourselves also know: [23] Him, being delivered by the determinate counsel and foreknowledge of God, ye have taken, and by wicked hands have crucified and slain: [24] Whom God hath raised up, having loosed the pains of death: because it was not possible that he should be holden of it."

Jesus was approved with miracles, signs and wonders by God, and all was consummated in His resurrection.

He's still performing miracles, signs and wonders today also because people are still debating, attacking and doubting His authenticity as the Saviour, if He's truly alive.

Jesus said some signs will follow His preachers and believers, as in Mark 16:15 "And he said unto them, Go ye into all the world, and preach the gospel to every creature. [16] He that believeth and is baptized shall be saved; but he that believeth not shall be damned. [17] And these signs shall follow them that believe; In my name shall they cast out devils; they shall speak with new tongues; [18] They shall take up serpents; and if they drink any deadly thing, it shall not hurt them; they shall lay hands on the sick, and they shall recover. [19] So then after the Lord had spoken unto them, he was received up into heaven, and sat on the right hand of God. [20] And they went forth, and preached every where, the Lord working with them, and confirming the word with signs following. Amen."

Because the Lord knows some people will still attack the authenticity of Jesus Christ and the Bible, He's confirming the signs He said would follow us.

People say the Bible was fabricated by "white people", but if the Bible was fabricated by them, are they also the ones that have entered our throats to speak in tongues; or to cast out devils; heal the sick etc, as stated would follow believers?

Do the supposed fabricators of the Bible have supernatural power to live in the believers of their fabrication to achieve supernatural feats?

God is intentional about these signs following us because the signs are also witnesses of the authenticity of His Son.

Some people also attack His resurrection but the operations of Apostles, Prophets, Evangelists, Pastors and Teachers are also witnesses of His resurrection because the Bible says He gave these gifts when He ascended on high by the resurrection.

THE DOCTRINE OF POWER; RIGHTLY DIVIDING THE SUPERNATURAL

It's one of the reasons these gifts haven't ceased in the church, for they're testament of His resurrection and ascension.

Every work of miracles, signs and wonders are witnesses of God.

The Lord said in John 5:36 "But I have greater witness than that of John: for the works which the Father hath given me to finish, the same works that I do, bear witness of me, that the Father hath sent me."

His works were consummated in His resurrection but the resurrection isn't the end of His miraculous power in the church.

Also, in John 10:25 "Jesus answered them, I told you, and ye believed not: the works that I do in my Father's name, they bear witness of me."

Again, in John 10:37 "If I do not the works of my Father, believe me not. [38] But if I do, though ye believe not me, believe the works: that ye may know, and believe, that the Father is in me, and I in him."

He further reiterated in John 14:10 "Believest thou not that I am in the Father, and the Father in me? the words that I speak unto you I speak not of myself: but the Father that dwelleth in me, he doeth the works. [11] Believe me that I am in the Father, and the Father in me: or else believe me for the very works' sake."

The Father works the words of the Son.

The preaching of the Gospel is in word and works, even spiritual works of the Holy Ghost.

So the Apostle said in 1 Corinthians 2:4 "And my speech and my preaching was not with enticing words of man's wisdom, but in demonstration of the Spirit and of power: [5] That your faith should not stand in the wisdom of men, but in the power of God."

In this same breath, it's said in 1 Corinthians 4:20 "For the kingdom of God is not in word, but in power."

Jesus is confirming the true story of His incarnation, crucifixion, burial and resurrection in the church today, also through present hour miracles, signs and wonders.

Divine works being witnesses for God and against those who see them and still remain ignorant willingly, the Lord Jesus said in John 15:22 "If I had not come and spoken unto them, they had not had sin: but now they have no cloke for their sin. [23] He that hateth me hateth my Father also. [24] If I had not done among them the works which none other man did, they had not had sin: but now have they both seen and hated both me and my Father."

Even if we run this down to the finished work, people still doubt the finished work so He's still doing miracles, signs and wonders as witnesses of the finished work.

In this same principle of witnesses without excuses, He said in Matthew 11:23 "And thou, Capernaum, which art exalted unto heaven, shalt be brought down to hell: for if the mighty works, which have been done in thee, had been done in Sodom, it would have remained until this day. [24] But I say unto you, That it shall be more tolerable for the land of Sodom in the day of judgment, than for thee."

THE DOCTRINE OF POWER; RIGHTLY DIVIDING THE SUPERNATURAL

If after confirming His finished work through the Church, people still choose to be ignorant of His authenticity, then they've no excuse!

This is why you can't write off His miracles, signs and wonders in this dispensation.

The writer of Hebrew said in Hebrews 2:3 "How shall we escape, if we neglect so great salvation; which at the first began to be spoken by the Lord, and was confirmed unto us by them that heard him ; [4] God also bearing them witness, both with signs and wonders, and with divers miracles, and gifts of the Holy Ghost, according to his own will?"

After the message of salvation has been confirmed with gifts of the Holy Spirit, divers miracles, signs and wonders, anyone who still hears the Gospel and say it's false or fabricated has no excuse!

He said these manifestations are by God's own will so no one has to be wiser than the will of God to say they're not needed.

When the Apostles were threatened, they prayed, as recorded in Acts 4:29 "And now, Lord, behold their threatenings: and grant unto thy servants, that with all boldness they may speak thy word, [30] By stretching forth thine hand to heal; and that signs and wonders may be done by the name of thy holy child Jesus. [31] And when they had prayed, the place was shaken where they were assembled together; and they were all filled with the Holy Ghost, and they spake the word of God with boldness. [33] And with great power gave the apostles witness of the resurrection of the Lord Jesus: and great grace was upon them all."

Giving witness to the resurrection with great power, is talking about the miracles, signs and wonders that followed them as they preach the Gospel.

People who despise miracles, signs and wonders use the excuse that believers don't need healing, etc.

However, believers also die bodily, and are going to be raised again by the manifestation of God's power, which is a sign and a wonder.

So far as the resurrection body has not been experientially consummated in believers, some will need to appropriate God's healing power in healing their bodies, just as the dead in Christ shall be raised, and those alive will be changed bodily.

Chapter 11

THE ORIGINAL SUPERNATURAL STATE

The supernatural is the original realm created for man.

God never intended that man walks in the flesh. The flesh is not the body in this perspective but anything that prevents the manifestation of the supernatural of God.

This concept of the flesh came when man fell.

This is why it is said in Genesis 6:3 that "And the LORD said, My spirit shall not always strive with man, for that he also is flesh: yet his days shall be an hundred and twenty years".

Man also is flesh.

It was not only man that was flesh but the whole creation, that is why it is said in 1 Corinthians 15:39 - "All flesh is not the same flesh: but there is one kind of flesh of men, another flesh of beasts, another of fishes, and another of birds".

All flesh here is not just man but all the living creatures.

So the biblical phrase, "all flesh is as grass" is talking about the fallen nature of all creation.

All creation were supposed to never wither or degenerate but the fall, so "the flower falls!"

The flower never had to fall but for the fall of man.

Thus, 1 Peter 1:24 - "For all flesh is as grass, and all the glory of man as the flower of grass. The grass withereth, and the flower thereof falleth away".

The body is different from the flesh in this perspective.

The flesh is a corruption and deviation from the very purpose of God, that is why it is said,

11 "The earth also was corrupt before God, and the earth was filled with violence.

12 And God looked upon the earth, and, behold, it was corrupt; for all flesh had corrupted his way upon the earth" (Genesis 6).

17 "And, behold, I, even I, do bring a flood of waters upon the earth, to destroy all flesh, wherein is the breath of life, from under heaven; and every thing that is in the earth shall die.

18 But with thee will I establish my covenant; and thou shalt come into the ark, thou, and thy sons, and thy wife, and thy sons' wives with thee.

19 And of every living thing of all flesh, two of every sort shalt thou bring into the ark, to keep them alive with thee; they shall be male and female" (Genesis 6).

All flesh is all the fallen creatures including man.

This is what the Prophet Isaiah, the Apostle Peter and the Prophet Joel were all referring to.

23 "Being born again, not of corruptible seed, but of incorruptible, by the word of God, which liveth and abideth for ever.

24 For all flesh is as grass, and all the glory of man as the flower of grass. The grass withereth, and the flower thereof falleth away:

25 But the word of the Lord endureth for ever. And this is the word which by the gospel is preached unto you" (1 Peter 1).

THE DOCTRINE OF POWER; RIGHTLY DIVIDING THE SUPERNATURAL

Peter is saying because all flesh is as grass because of the fall, and God had said that His Spirit would not always strive with man, now that God is regenerating and reconciling all things back to His original plan and position, He is doing it through the preaching of the word!

"For all flesh is as grass, and all the glory of man as the flower of grass. The grass withereth, and the flower thereof falleth away:

But the word of the Lord endureth for ever. And this is the word which by the gospel is preached unto you".

All flesh will not endure forever but the Word of the Lord will, so God is using the word to recreate all flesh so that they will come into their original place of eternal glory and not remain as the flower that falls.

"Being born again, not of corruptible seed, but of incorruptible, by the word of God, which liveth and abideth for ever".

This new birth is contrary to the fallen flesh.

3 "Jesus answered and said unto him, Verily, verily, I say unto thee, Except a man be born again, he cannot see the kingdom of God.

4 Nicodemus saith unto him, How can a man be born when he is old? can he enter the second time into his mother's womb, and be born?

5 Jesus answered, Verily, verily, I say unto thee, Except a man be born of water and of the Spirit, he cannot enter into the kingdom of God" (John 3).

The flesh and blood that "man fell to", must be born again, this time not of flesh but of the Spirit and water, where the Water is the Word which Peter says has been preached unto us.

This is what the Apostle James has said, "Of his own will begat he us with the word of truth, that we should be a kind of firstfruits of his creatures" (James 1:18).

By the Word we have been born again, not as corruptible flesh but of incorruptible seed!

John said,

11 "He came unto his own, and his own received him not.

12 But as many as received him, to them gave he power to become the sons of God, even to them that believe on his name:

13 Which were born, not of blood, nor of the will of the flesh, nor of the will of man, but of God" (John 1).

They are now born of God who is a Spirit as spirit and not as flesh so that they can now see and inherit the kingdom of God.

1 Corinthians 15:50 says, "Now this I say, brethren, that flesh and blood cannot inherit the kingdom of God; neither doth corruption inherit incorruption".

The Kingdom was God's original purpose for man, but man would not enter it with a fallen nature which is flesh so man must be born again.

The Lord Jesus demonstrated to us that spiritual flesh which man was supposed to have, which is His resurrection body.

It is said in Hebrews 2:14 - "Forasmuch then as the children are partakers of flesh and blood, he also himself likewise took part of the same; that through death he might destroy him that had the power of death, that is, the devil".

THE DOCTRINE OF POWER; RIGHTLY DIVIDING THE SUPERNATURAL

The human race, are the children who fell from their glorious body to become flesh and blood so the Lord also left His glory behind and partook in the same flesh and blood in order to bring the children back into their original place of glory!

In His resurrection, when the disciples were doubting Him, He said, even in Luke 24:39 - "Behold my hands and my feet, that it is I myself: handle me, and see; for a spirit hath not flesh and bones, as ye see me have".

So the Lord in His resurrection doesn't have a fallen flesh and blood but rather the original spiritual flesh and bones that man was supposed to become before the fall.

There is something called spiritual flesh which is also the spiritual body.

It is this same spiritual flesh and body that is called glorious body.

"Who shall change our vile body, that it may be fashioned like unto his glorious body, according to the working whereby he is able even to subdue all things unto himself" (Philippians 3:21).

This is the body the Lord Jesus resurrected with.

Job said in Job 14:1 that "Man that is born of a woman is of few days and full of trouble".

But being born again, we are no longer born of women, but of God.

"Which were born, not of blood, nor of the will of the flesh, nor of the will of man, but of God" (John 1:13).

Also in 1 Peter 1:23 - "Being born again, not of corruptible seed, but of incorruptible, by the word of God, which liveth and abideth for ever".

We are no longer of few days and full of trouble.

John 5:24 says, "Verily, verily, I say unto you, He that heareth my word, and believeth on him that sent me, hath everlasting life, and shall not come into condemnation; but is passed from death unto life."

We are of eternal life, full of grace and truth just like the Lord Jesus.

"For both he that sanctifieth and they who are sanctified are all of one: for which cause he is not ashamed to call them brethren" (Hebrews 2:11).

This reality and consciousness makes us explore our supernatural state in Christ, manifesting beyond the limitations of the fallen flesh and blood.

We're born again by the eternal word of God to live forever.

THE DOCTRINE OF POWER; RIGHTLY DIVIDING THE SUPERNATURAL

Exploring "huperballō"

The resurrection of Christ is the greatest demonstration of God's power, showcasing His sovereignty over life, death, and all creation. It conquered death, the ultimate enemy of humanity, and reversed the natural order of decay and entropy, restoring Jesus' body to a glorified, imperishable state. This supernatural event transcends the laws of nature to prove God's authority over the physical world.

The resurrection also fulfilled ancient prophecies and God's promises, demonstrating His faithfulness and power to accomplish His purposes. Through this event, God demonstrated His power to redeem and save humanity, offering eternal life and reconciliation with Himself. The resurrection authenticates Jesus' claims and teachings, confirming His divinity and authority as the Son of God.

In the resurrection, we see the highest power, a power that no creature had ever seen before, a power that transcends human and angelic comprehension, and a power that gives us hope and assurance of our own redemption and eternal life. It is the revelation of God's omnipotence, omniscience, and ultimately, His love; a reminder of His intimate involvement in the human experience.

The Greek word for "resurrection power" is "Dunamis", which means "power", "strength", "ability", or "miraculous power". In the context of the resurrection, it refers to the mighty and miraculous power of God that raised Jesus Christ from the dead.

In the New Testament, Dunamis is used to describe the power of God that:

Raised Jesus from the dead (Ephesians 1:19-20, Philippians 3:10);

Gives believers new life and resurrection power (Romans 6:4-5, Ephesians 2:1-6);

- Enables believers to live a victorious life (Philippians 4:13, Colossians 1:29).

Another related Greek word is "Exousia" which means "authority" or "power". This word is often used in conjunction with "Dunamis" to emphasize the authority and power of God.

These Greek words help us understand the magnitude and significance of the resurrection power that is available to us through faith in Jesus Christ!

Let us consider Ephesians 1:19 - "And what is the exceeding greatness of his power to us-ward who believe, according to the working of his mighty power,.."

Let's explore the Greek words in this verse, starting with "exceeding" which is "huperballō", which means to throw beyond the usual mark". By implication, the greatness of the power in us is beyond the usual mark, such that when men hear of it in manifestation, they'll only conclude it as an exaggeration. The Greek says "huperballō megethos autos dunamis..."

The far surpassing, supereminent magnitude of His resurrection power in us!

Comparing the glory of the Old Testament with that of the new, the Spirit used huperballō in 2 Corinthians 3:10 "For even that which was made glorious had no glory in this respect, by reason of the glory that excelleth (huperballō)".

He's saying our glory is thrown beyond the usual mark; it Super abounds! It's supereminent! It far surpasses in the infinitive! It's huperballō; it doesn't diminish but only superabounds in intensity and dimensions in proportion to God's essential essence!

The word is also used in Ephesians 2:7 - "That in the ages to come he might shew the exceeding (huperballō) riches of his grace in his kindness toward us through Christ Jesus."

His grace has riches, and every riches of His grace is "huperballōd". This is the infinitive dimensions of our God! Every grace in you has various riches, dimensions., which are "huperballōd", thrown beyond the usual mark in supereminent fashion.

The healing grace in you can manifest in another/higher fashion! The tongues you speak can take on a far richer dimension.

It's said in 2 Corinthians 9:14 - "And by their prayer for you, which long after you for the exceeding (huperballō) grace of God in you."

The grace of God in us is thrown beyond the usual mark.

Once again, it's such that when in full expression, people who hear of it will conclude it to be an exaggeration.

This is why you can't determine the manifestation of grace by what you're used to, saying this is how God has been moving so if He moves in another dimension or fashion then it's not God.

His grace and its riches in us and for us is huperballō.

His power and love in us and for us are same, huperballō! We live in the glory which "huperballōs"!

Why do you think you can put God and His dimensions (riches of His grace) in a box by your carnal mind and limited experiences?

When it's even said that God does beyond our wildest imagination and thoughts? Thus, Ephesians 3:20 - "Now unto him that is able to do exceeding abundantly above all that we ask or think, according to the power that worketh in us,".

It's in the Greek as huperekperissou from huper = above + ek = intensifies meaning, adding idea of exhaustlessness + perissos = exceeding some number or measure, over and above, more than necessary; means surpassing, superabundantly, surpassingly, beyond measure, exceedingly, quite beyond all measure, overwhelming, over and above, more than enough. It describes an extraordinary degree, involving a considerable excess over what would be expected, beyond the finite and carnal mind!

We've to be careful what we conclude as final in God's supernatural manifestation and moves, understanding that some things may not be explicitly mentioned, listed or stated in the Bible but still layered linguistically in the Word for us to explore by the Spirit of truth.

Expand the scope of your consciousness in proportion to the greatness of God by the Spirit of Truth!

Chapter 12

Beyond the false standard in the infantile Church

The Apostle John has written concerning Jesus Christ in Revelation 1:14 - "His head and his hairs were white like wool, as white as snow; and his eyes were as a flame of fire; 15 And his feet like unto fine brass, as if they burned in a furnace; and his voice as the sound of many waters."

After he saw this, he came and wrote in 1 John 3:2 - "Beloved, now are we the sons of God, and it doth not yet appear what we shall be: but we know that, when he shall appear, we shall be like him; for we shall see him as he is."

For who we shall be like, we know we'll be like Him but it does not yet appear what we'll be like!

The untapped divine potentials in us are far greater than all angelic powers put together.

Some people have prejudice against the supernatural in Christ because they've a certain mindset about the scope of man's spirituality. To them the supernatural is just laying hands and people fall then we celebrate few healings then that's all.

If that's all there's to the supernatural in Christ then Christ is limited, and all power and authority doesn't belong to Him!

But thanks be to God that Christ indeed has all power, and God is the source of all powers.

As we've been seeing, there's no power that belongs to the devil and there's no ability that the devil and the rebellious beings have monopoly over; every power belongs to God Almighty; the rebellious beings use God's power outside original intent and purpose and that's what makes it evil, as evil is that which is out of original intent and purpose. Evil is that which chooses to be sufficient by itself and not be sufficient of God the essential source.

As we've considered before, the fact that a third of the angels rebelled and use their initial, God-given powers and abilities out of purpose doesn't mean God has lost such powers and abilities in Himself.

God's glory which is the sum total of His essence can never be diminished; that's to say, God can give you something out of Himself yet that aspect has never diminished in Him. All the powers and abilities in the rebellious beings are much more in God according to their original purpose and intention.

When people who don't understand this perspective see a harmless demonstration of power by sons of God beyond their scope of knowledge and understanding then they conclude it as being of the devil.

These same people don't have a problem when angels appear like men, when Jesus who's currently in man's glorified body goes through walls, levitates, transmogrifies; changes Himself to the point that even His disciples couldn't recognize Him, His eyes burn with literal fire as a man, etc, but they conclude His brethren who're being conformed to His image to be devilish, etc, just because of little portion of His power manifesting in them.

THE DOCTRINE OF POWER; RIGHTLY DIVIDING THE SUPERNATURAL

How one discerns can't go beyond his prejudice and spiritual understanding. We must not mistake "prejudiced-suspicion" to mean discerning.

Until the overcomers attain this level of understanding and consciousness they may not go beyond the false standard currently in the infantile church.

The glorious church is the church of the word and power.

Once again, 1 John 3:2 - "Beloved, now are we the sons of God, and it doth not yet appear what we shall be: but we know that, when he shall appear, we shall be like him; for we shall see him as he is."

It does not yet appear what we shall be! It's growth into Christ, into God; what I call the Immanuel counsel!

The dynamics of the power of sonship which is equality with the Father are being unlocked in us according to the scope of our understanding.

Multifarious Operations of Christ

To go far in your pursuit of God in His knowledge in Christ, don't make any man of God your standard; don't make any denomination your standard; don't make any "move of God" your standard. You can learn from them but they're not the last stop or yardstick in measuring God's greatness.

I tell people that the churches in America, Europe, Africa, Asia, etc, are not the standard of the Universal Church of Jesus Christ.

Some people in Africa, for example, may watch the churches in America and other places, and try to use them as yardstick for the church in Africa. Some people in the churches in America may also watch the churches in Africa and try to use themselves as standard to judge them.

The way the Churches in America pray aren't the standard of prayer for the universal church; the way a particular man of God prays isn't the standard for praying for all believers.

Some people say the early church in the book of Acts is the standard of the universal church of Jesus Christ. However, that's half truth. The church in the book of Acts was the infantile Church. The Church was just born, and they're trying to find their way to the standard of Christ, in accurate knowledge and power.

They had issues over doctrines; exclusion or inclusion of Gentile believers etc.

Some were mixing law and grace, which is dangerous.

The early church wasn't the standard of the universal church, both in doctrine and operations of the power of God.

What and Who is the standard of the universal Church?

It's "The Son of Man; the Christ, the Son of the Living God".

Thus, Matthew 16:16 "And Simon Peter answered and said, Thou art the Christ, the Son of the living God. [17] And Jesus answered and said unto him, Blessed art thou, Simon Barjona: for flesh and blood hath not revealed it unto thee, but my Father which is in heaven. [18] And I say also unto thee, That thou art Peter, and upon this rock I will build my church; and the gates of hell shall not prevail against it."

THE DOCTRINE OF POWER; RIGHTLY DIVIDING THE SUPERNATURAL

"The Son of Man; the Christ, the Son of the Living God" is the foundation, the superstructure, the cornerstone, the material, the standard of the universal church.

He's the universality of God, multifaceted, multidimensional, multifarious, the one but expressing Himself diversely, unique in all unto one purpose. No one person has monopoly of Him.

He's quiet in some but loud in others, as He's the Creator of quietness and loudness. So the fact that you've a quiet approach to prayer doesn't mean you should see others who are loud as ignorant folks.

He's calm in some but roars in others.

He's unique in everyone. He's the standard of the Church.

Ephesians 4:11 says, "And he gave some, apostles; and some, prophets; and some, evangelists; and some, pastors and teachers; [12] For the perfecting of the saints, for the work of the ministry, for the edifying of the body of Christ: [13] Till we all come in the unity of the faith, and of the knowledge of the Son of God, unto a perfect man, unto the measure of the stature of the fulness of Christ:".

The Standard is the Son of God, a perfect man, the measure of the stature of the fullness of Christ.

The verses, 15 "But speaking the truth in love, may grow up into him in all things, which is the head, even Christ: [16] From whom the whole body fitly joined together and compacted by that which every joint supplieth, according to the effectual working in the measure of every part, maketh increase of the body unto the edifying of itself in love."

Every joint supply something unique to the body, and we grow up into Him in all things. He's in all things and all things are in Him.

Once again, how American churches pray, prophesy and heal the sick among others aren't the standard for the universal church. The same way, how African churches do theirs isn't the standard either. Christ is the standard, and He's multifarious.

We learn from one another but no one is the standard.

Some men of God who may be mentored by some American preachers may look down on the unique manifestations of Christ in Africa because they may esteem the Americans as the standard.

What Is The Foundation Of Apostles And Prophets?

Let's explore Ephesians 2:18-22 "For through him we both have access by one Spirit unto the Father. Now therefore ye are no more strangers and foreigners, but fellowcitizens with the saints, and of the household of God; And are built upon the foundation of the apostles and prophets, Jesus Christ himself being the chief corner stone ; In whom all the building fitly framed together groweth unto an holy temple in the Lord: In whom ye also are builded together for an habitation of God through the Spirit."

THE DOCTRINE OF POWER; RIGHTLY DIVIDING THE SUPERNATURAL

Some people use the above verses to attack supernatural manifestations in the Church, saying that if it's not recorded in the book of Acts that people fell under the power of God during ministrations, for example, then it's not part of the foundation of the Apostles and Prophets.

From the import of the verses, and the revelation of Christ in the Bible, the foundation of the Apostles and Prophets is beyond what the early Apostles and Prophets did in the book of Acts. Christ Jesus is the only foundation, and no one can lay any other foundation beside Him or in addition to Him. He's the foundation of the Apostles and Prophets. It means all their doctrines and manifestations of power stemmed out of Him, thus expressing His multifarious wisdom and power.

In essence, the foundation of the Apostles and Prophets is Christ-centered, and any supernatural manifestations or teachings that align with His character, wisdom, and power, thus through the lens of His finished work, is part of this foundation.

The Apostles and Prophets in the book of Acts, had such a short period, coupled with too much persecutions to be able to explore the fullness of Christ, to be recorded.

When we refer to Jesus Christ, we're encompassing His complete nature, including His wisdom, power, and gifts. His gifts, such as eternal life, righteousness, healing, prophecy, and more, are all integral parts of who He is as the foundation.

In essence, His gifts are not separate from Him but are extensions of His character, wisdom, and power. This is the unity and completeness of Christ as the foundation of our faith.

By recognizing that His gifts are part of Him, we acknowledge that everything we receive from Him is rooted in His nature and character. This understanding encourages us to embrace the fullness of Christ and His gifts, knowing that they are all connected to His wisdom and power.

"Show me where Jesus or the Apostles operated like that in the Bible"

There are times, we manifest some gifts and operations of the Holy Spirit and people "prejudicedly" ask, "where in the Bible is it written or recorded?" Some even say Jesus didn't operate like that so it's not from God.

All dimensions of God in Christ cannot be written, itemized or recorded in "the Bible". However, they're compressed into words, phrases and statements to be opened up in us, in our everyday lives, in line with truth.

"And there are also many other things which Jesus did, the which, if they should be written every one, I suppose that even the world itself could not contain the books that should be written. Amen" (John 21:25).

In many accounts, how Jesus operated or manifested His power wasn't detailed or itemized, yet He operated diversely.

There were times He spoke the word only and things happened.

THE DOCTRINE OF POWER; RIGHTLY DIVIDING THE SUPERNATURAL

There were times people touched His garment and were healed, as in Mark 6:55 "And ran through that whole region round about, and began to carry about in beds those that were sick, where they heard he was. [56] And whithersoever he entered, into villages, or cities, or country, they laid the sick in the streets, and besought him that they might touch if it were but the border of his garment: and as many as touched him were made whole."

There were times He only lifted by the hand without saying anything, as in Mark 1:31 "And he came and took her by the hand, and lifted her up; and immediately the fever left her, and she ministered unto them."

Someone ministering with the hand without talking, yet things are happening isn't new, and shouldn't be a strange thing. It's called signs, and every sign has meanings, even spiritual communication that involves the interaction of spiritual power.

Matthew 4:24 says, "And his fame went throughout all Syria: and they brought unto him all sick people that were taken with divers diseases and torments, and those which were possessed with devils, and those which were lunatick, and those that had the palsy; and he healed them."

Again, it's not revealed the various modes of healings He operated, whether or not He laid hands on the lunatics or He caused them to fall by moving His feet, yet the Bible talks about "gifts of healings", "plural gifts of plural healings".

Thus, 1 Corinthians 12:28 "And God hath set some in the church, first apostles, secondarily prophets, thirdly teachers, after that miracles, then gifts of healings,..[30] Have all the gifts of healing?.." or 1 Corinthians 12:9 "To another faith by the same Spirit; to another the gifts of healing by the same Spirit;".

"Gifts of healing(s)" means there are various modes of operating the same gift; some blow air, some lay hands, some shadow, some use the eyes, some shake their bodies, some dance etc. Jesus who's given these gifts should also operate in all Himself.

In the acts of the Apostles and the early Church, the Bible hasn't always detailed how they operated or manifested, it only summarized the things that occurred.

The Scriptures provide a foundation for our faith, but they don't exhaustively document every detail of their actions and methods.

It's not an exhaustive manual that checks every milliseconds of our everyday lives and operations.

For instance, Acts 15:12 "Then all the multitude kept silence, and gave audience to Barnabas and Paul, declaring what miracles and wonders God had wrought among the Gentiles by them."

It didn't reveal the various ways the miracles and wonders happened through them, yet we know that it's not "one way" but diverse, even as said in 1 Corinthians 12:4 "Now there are diversities of gifts, but the same Spirit. [5] And there are differences of administrations, but the same Lord. [6] And there are diversities of operations, but it is the same God which worketh all in all."

THE DOCTRINE OF POWER; RIGHTLY DIVIDING THE SUPERNATURAL

Acts 6:8 says, "And Stephen, full of faith and power, did great wonders and miracles among the people."

Stephen's great wonders and miracles aren't itemized, let alone how they happened.

2 Corinthians 12:12 says, "Truly the signs of an apostle were wrought among you in all patience, in signs, and wonders, and mighty deeds."

1 Corinthians 2:4 says, "And my speech and my preaching was not with enticing words of man's wisdom, but in demonstration of the Spirit and of power: [5] That your faith should not stand in the wisdom of men, but in the power of God."

Galatians 3:5 says, "He therefore that ministereth to you the Spirit, and worketh miracles among you, doeth he it by the works of the law, or by the hearing of faith?"

All the above and other verses show miracles, signs and wonders happening in the churches yet aren't explicitly itemized, so the next time you want to "attack" a harmless manifestation of the Spirit just because it's beyond your understanding, asking where it's written in the Bible, you should first know the Bible hasn't detailed how all miracles, signs, wonders and manifestations of the Spirit happened.

Let's also explore 1 Corinthians 12:4 "Now there are diversities of gifts, but the same Spirit. [5] And there are differences of administrations, but the same Lord. [6] And there are diversities of operations, but it is the same God which worketh all in all."

The Greek word for "operations" in this verse is "energēma", which is from the word, "energeō", which means to "be mighty in", "show forth (one's) self" as used in Matthew 14:1 "At that time Herod the tetrarch heard of the fame of Jesus, [2] And said unto his servants, This is John the Baptist; he is risen from the dead; and therefore mighty works do shew forth themselves in him."

What it means is that mighty works were showing forth themselves in Jesus so much that His fame reached Herod, but he assumed Jesus was John whom he beheaded.

So, in diversities of operations, mighty works show forth themselves in people, according to the wisdom of God.

It's same word that's used as "wrought effectually", and "mighty in", in Galatians 2:8 "(For he that wrought effectually in Peter to the apostleship of the circumcision, the same was mighty in me toward the Gentiles:)".

There were varieties of operations in Peter and Paul, in both the ministration of the Word and power, but it's the same God.

Going further into the root word, it even speaks of giving oneself wholly, implying that God can use every part of one's body to accomplish His purpose.

Some say "why do you use every part of your body to minister?"

That's because God created the body for His purpose so knows how to use every part for His purpose. The body is the temple of the Holy Spirit so He can use it as He wants.

THE DOCTRINE OF POWER; RIGHTLY DIVIDING THE SUPERNATURAL

We look at the principle of the members of the body being instrument of righteousness, as in Romans 6:13 "Neither yield ye your members as instruments of unrighteousness unto sin: but yield yourselves unto God, as those that are alive from the dead, and your members as instruments of righteousness unto God."

"Instruments" in this verse is also "weapons" in the Greek.

Which implies that every part of the body is a weapon.

Any spirit can use any part of the body depending on which spirit a person yields it to; the spirit of witchcraft uses the eyes, hands, feet, tongue and every other part for evil/sin.

But we yield the members of our bodies to the Holy Spirit as weapons of righteousness, even in spiritual manifestations.

I take another query principle from Psalm 94:9 "He that planted the ear, shall he not hear? he that formed the eye, shall he not see? [10] He that chastiseth the heathen, shall not he correct? he that teacheth man knowledge, shall not he know ?"

Why shouldn't the true Creator of the body know how to use its members best, according to His wisdom and purpose?

I'm a yielded creature to the Almighty, All-knowing, Only Wise Creator, even Jesus Christ of Nazareth!

Falling Under the Power

There are people who talk down on people falling during spiritual ministrations in the Church.

There are so many reasons this happen.

We see from Genesis, the book of beginnings, how God caused Adam to fall asleep, as in Genesis 2:21 "And the Lord God caused a deep sleep to fall upon Adam, and he slept: and he took one of his ribs, and closed up the flesh instead thereof;".

The Hebrew word for "caused" is "nâphal", which also means to cause to fall, fell, throw down, knock out, lay prostrate, etc.

By implication, Adam's situation was unique but the concept and manifestation didn't cease with him.

For example, Abraham was also put to sleep by God in Genesis 15:12 "And when the sun was going down, a deep sleep fell upon Abram; and, lo, an horror of great darkness fell upon him."

There are various forms of falling under the power, which all have specific meanings, as they're all signs.

It's said in 2 Chronicles 5:14, how the tangible glory of God manifested, "So that the priests could not stand to minister by reason of the cloud: for the glory of the Lord had filled the house of God."

When the Apostles prayed in Acts 4:29-31 "And now, Lord, behold their threatenings: and grant unto thy servants, that with all boldness they may speak thy word, By stretching forth thine hand to heal; and that signs and wonders may be done by the name of thy holy child Jesus. And when they had prayed, the place was shaken where they were assembled together; and they were all filled with the Holy Ghost, and they spake the word of God with boldness."

The Greek word for "shaken" in the verse is "saleuō", which also means "to be shaken together with its content".

THE DOCTRINE OF POWER; RIGHTLY DIVIDING THE SUPERNATURAL

By implication, the Apostles fell down when the place was shaken.

People fall under the power when there's a spiritual shaking, in their systems, sometimes during ministrations of healing, signs and wonders.

The physical sign of falling under the power is a manifestation of our surrender and humility in response to God's mighty presence and power. When we fall, it's a sign acknowledging that God's power is beyond our control, and our bodies respond in a way that reflects our reverence and awe.

In that moment, we're reminded that God is in charge, and we're not. We're humbled by the experience, and our pride and self-sufficiency are laid aside. It's a sign of expression of worship, as our bodies and spirits surrender to His majesty.

This physical act also represents a spiritual surrender. We're yielding our will, our strength, and our control to God, acknowledging that He is the One who holds all power and authority. It's a declaration that we trust Him completely, and we're willing to be vulnerable and open to His work in our lives.

When we fall under the power, we're also experiencing a tangible manifestation of God's presence and power. It's a sensory experience that can't be ignored or denied. Our bodies are responding to a spiritual reality that's beyond our comprehension, and it's a powerful reminder that God is real, present, and active in our lives.

In that moment, we're experientially united with God in a profound way, and our faith is strengthened. We're reminded that we're not alone, and God is always with us, guiding and empowering us. Falling under the power is a beautiful expression of our dependence on God and our trust in His goodness and love.

Chapter 13

Wisdom of prayer beyond carnal analysis

There are many kinds of prayers but let's explore some specific expressions of the Spirit in prayer. There are people who always attack other Christians on certain kinds of groanings and monosyllabic expressions in prayer.

Spiritual things are not carnally discerned, as said in 1 Corinthians 2:14 - "But the natural man receiveth not the things of the Spirit of God: for they are foolishness unto him: neither can he know them, because they are spiritually discerned."

There are carnal Christians who always analyze spiritual things carnally; they use their minds to direct the way they pray with the spirit so it can sound nice and sweet to the ear but praying in tongues isn't "beauty or sweetness contest."

For proper spiritual growth and development you just have to yield to the Holy Spirit by opening your mouth and let Him give you utterances; with this, whether He's giving you monosyllabic sounds you just keep on till He changes them Himself, as expressed in Romans 8:26 - "Likewise the Spirit also helpeth our infirmities: for we know not what we should pray for as we ought: but the Spirit itself maketh intercession for us with groanings which cannot be uttered."

There's a place we groan in the Spirit beyond intellectual comprehension. We don't have to be so caught up in intellectualism that we become even wiser than the Holy Spirit in His expressions in prayer.

There's a kind of tongues we speak for interpretation and there's a kind of tongues which is prayer language for self-edification in the Spirit, as Jude 1:20 says "But ye, beloved, building up yourselves on your most holy faith, praying in the Holy Ghost,".

This is building up ourselves like a high-rising building. There's a realm of prayer in the Spirit where you're not necessarily praying to God to respond with words but you're just building up yourself in Him and with Him! It's a spiritual exercise; it's participating in the Divine experience, not praying to God but praying with Him!

There's another dimension of praying with the spirit in the Spirit that you're aligning things by your authority in the name of Jesus Christ. The spiritual life is so huge beyond natural comprehension.

What seems like monosyllabic naturally doesn't necessarily mean repetitive in the Spirit.

Language is complex, and meanings can vary across languages and dialects.

In the spiritual realm, a single word or sound can carry multiple layers of meaning, and the Holy Spirit can use even the simplest expressions to convey profound truths and emotions. It's essential to approach spiritual language with an open heart and mind, recognizing that God's language is often beyond human comprehension.

There are words with same spelling in various languages and dialects but have different meanings.

THE DOCTRINE OF POWER; RIGHTLY DIVIDING THE SUPERNATURAL

We know about words that are spelled the same, but have different meanings, and words that are spelled differently, but sound the same. These are homophones, homographs and homonyms.

God made them so, as the Creator of all things.

Similarly, in the spiritual realm, a single expression can hold multiple meanings and significance.

In spiritual intelligence, God can make a sound and multitudes would hear it differently. So Psalm 62:11 says, "God hath spoken once; twice have I heard this; that power belongeth unto God."

God can also speak once and we'd hear it multiple times and with diverse, accurate understanding.

A sound has manifold expressions and interpretations by the Wisdom of God.

An angel can sound a trumpet and it's saying so many things.

God Himself queried Job in Job 40:9 - "Hast thou an arm like God? or canst thou thunder with a voice like him?"

When God speaks this way, to the natural and carnal man it's just a sound without meaning but to the one initiated into that realm of understanding it's a whole conversation. The principle of praying in God the Holy Spirit is also a principle of sounds!

We've seen an instance in John 12, where the Father spoke to Jesus but those present heard it differently, thus verses, 28 "Father, glorify thy name. Then came there a voice from heaven, saying, I have both glorified it, and will glorify it again.

29 The people therefore, that stood by, and heard it, said that it thundered: others said, An angel spake to him.

30 Jesus answered and said, This voice came not because of me, but for your sakes."

What actually happened carnally was a thunder but it's a voice and utterance of the Father, which the Son understood very well but those present had different interpretations.

One utterance, one sound in the Spirit can have ten thousand expressions in the realm of God.

We've seen similar thing in Daniel 5:25 - "And this is the writing that was written, MENE, MENE, TEKEL, UPHARSIN.

26 This is the interpretation of the thing: MENE; God hath numbered thy kingdom, and finished it.

27 TEKEL; Thou art weighed in the balances, and art found wanting.

28 PERES; Thy kingdom is divided, and given to the Medes and Persians."

When you study this strange tongue and the interpretation, you'll realize spiritual things are not carnally discerned!

Maybe to you someone's prayer in tongues doesn't make sense, it's monosyllabic, it's not sweet cascading, it's foolishness but to God it's spiritually meaningful!

Every sound from the instruments we play in God's presence can be understood in the Spirit; to the carnal mind it's just nice music.

The Psalmist knowing this would say, in Psalm 150:3 - "Praise him with the sound of the trumpet: praise him with the psaltery and harp.

4 Praise him with the timbrel and dance: praise him with stringed instruments and organs."

THE DOCTRINE OF POWER; RIGHTLY DIVIDING THE SUPERNATURAL

If sounds from instruments can be understood in the Spirit then any sound or groaning in the Spirit by believers can be meaningfully discerned!

God's wisdom in prayer is so vast that even prayer is represented in heaven like odours, smoke, incense, thus Revelation 5:8 - "And when he had taken the book, the four beasts and four and twenty elders fell down before the Lamb, having every one of them harps, and golden vials full of odours, which are the prayers of saints."

If prayers can be represented and interpreted in heaven in smoke then any sound in prayer in the Spirit can be meaningfully interpreted in God and by God.

Some people say God isn't deaf so we don't need to shout in prayer. However, we know God Himself shouts! There's a place for quiet prayer, and that of loud prayer. This is a God who knows every thought before they're uttered yet He's also established the principle of praying, and shouting in prayer. If we want to be carnally logical without following God's principle, it'll mean we shouldn't pray at all since He already knows all things.

Jesus Himself shouted in prayer as said in Hebrews 5:7 - "Who in the days of his flesh, when he had offered up prayers and supplications with strong crying and tears unto him that was able to save him from death, and was heard in that he feared;" the word "strong" here is the Greek, "ischuros" which also means boisterous, powerful, mighty; Jesus prayed boisterously when He walked the earth.

Let's stop being carnal in the name of being gentle and sweet!

Jesus called forth Lazarus with a loud voice!

Thus, John 11:43-44 "And when he thus had spoken, he cried with a loud voice, Lazarus, come forth. And he that was dead came forth, bound hand and foot with graveclothes: and his face was bound about with a napkin. Jesus saith unto them, Loose him, and let him go."

There are people who say "why are all believers shouting in prayer? It's a confused gathering", but we know God cannot be confused no matter the number of people talking at the same time! He's already watching and hearing every single person everywhere in the universe or multiverse, at the same time, knowing all their thoughts and actions, yet they're not noisy to Him, so it's not the corporate prayer gathering that would now make Him confused!

After all, out of His own throne proceeds thunderings and voices! Thus Revelation 4:5 - "And out of the throne proceeded lightnings and thunderings and voices: and there were seven lamps of fire burning before the throne, which are the seven Spirits of God."

His own voice is as the sound of many waters, as in Revelation 1:15 "And his feet like unto fine brass, as if they burned in a furnace; and his voice as the sound of many waters." Which is connection with Ezekiel 43:2 "And, behold, the glory of the God of Israel came from the way of the east: and his voice was like a noise of many waters: and the earth shined with his glory."

In ancient Jewish literature, the "sound of many waters" was a common phrase used to describe the roar of a large crowd or the sound of a mighty ocean.

Our corporate voices are just like an expression of His single voice!

Let's be wise with God and not the wisdom of carnal men, so we can fully explore the dimensions and realms in God that are originally ordained for us in Christ.

Chapter 14

The Ever-Abiding Holy Spirit

Now, let's explore John 14:16 "And I will pray the Father, and he shall give you another Comforter, that he may abide with you for ever; [17] Even the Spirit of truth; whom the world cannot receive, because it seeth him not, neither knoweth him: but ye know him; for he dwelleth with you, and shall be in you."

There's been teachings that created consciousness in people that the Holy Spirit leaves a believer in Christ when he commits sins.

This is rather misrepresenting the Holy Spirit, that He's not able to accomplish His assignment in the believer, which is based on the finished work of Christ.

We don't set aside the authority of the scriptures, which is consummated in the finished work of Christ and start teaching our own wisdom.

The Holy Spirit as another Comforter, is another of the same kind of Jesus Christ.

When Jesus was talking to them at that time He said that they knew the Spirit of Truth because He dwells with them then and shall be in them.

Jesus was talking about Himself as the Spirit of Truth who they know and was dwelling with them, and shall be in them in another of the same kind, the Holy Spirit.

THE DOCTRINE OF POWER; RIGHTLY DIVIDING THE SUPERNATURAL

The Holy Spirit has come in the name of the Lord Jesus Christ, which means He's working in and with the believer according to the finished work of Christ, and He'll not leave anyone that Jesus has saved by faith in Him.

It's the finished work of Christ that opened the veil for the Spirit to come in the first place, as said in John 7:37 "In the last day, that great day of the feast, Jesus stood and cried, saying, If any man thirst, let him come unto me, and drink. [38] He that believeth on me, as the scripture hath said, out of his belly shall flow rivers of living water. [39] (But this spake he of the Spirit, which they that believe on him should receive: for the Holy Ghost was not yet given ; because that Jesus was not yet glorified.)"

The Spirit was only given when Jesus was glorified in His death, burial and resurrection.

The Holy Spirit is living in and with the believer, not by self-righteousness and works of the believer but solely by faith in Jesus Christ.

The Apostle Paul by the Spirit would say in Galatians 3:2 "This only would I learn of you, Received ye the Spirit by the works of the law, or by the hearing of faith? [3] Are ye so foolish? having begun in the Spirit, are ye now made perfect by the flesh? [5] He therefore that ministereth to you the Spirit, and worketh miracles among you, doeth he it by the works of the law, or by the hearing of faith?"

We receive the Spirit by the hearing of faith, which is the Gospel of the death, burial and resurrection of Jesus Christ; we began in the Gospel of faith and are perfected by the Gospel of faith.

It's not the works of the flesh that enabled us to receive the Spirit so it's not the works of the flesh that sustain Him or cause Him to leave a believer.

The Father, the Son and the Holy Spirit have one mind and purpose, to redeem creation to the uttermost through the finished work of Christ Jesus.

Let's not misrepresent this counsel by our contrary wisdom.

People say that any believer who commits sins and still speaks in tongues and operates in other gifts of the Spirit is lying; it's not the Holy Spirit that's operating in the person.

These people think so because as I keep saying, their wisdom is carnal; "do good, get good philosophy", and it's contrary to God's wisdom of redemption in Christ.

As we've seen in above, Apostle Paul asked in Galatians 3:2 "This only would I learn of you, Received ye the Spirit by the works of the law, or by the hearing of faith? [3] Are ye so foolish? having begun in the Spirit, are ye now made perfect by the flesh? [5] He therefore that ministereth to you the Spirit, and worketh miracles among you, doeth he it by the works of the law, or by the hearing of faith?"

We receive the Spirit by faith in the finished work of Christ, and the Spirit abides in and with us in same faith.

He said working of miracles, and all other gifts and works of the Spirit in and through the believer is by the hearing of faith, which is salvation by faith in the death, burial and resurrection of Jesus Christ.

It's not by one's own qualification or perfection.

THE DOCTRINE OF POWER; RIGHTLY DIVIDING THE SUPERNATURAL

It's said in Colossians 2:6 "As ye have therefore received Christ Jesus the Lord, so walk ye in him: [7] Rooted and built up in him, and stablished in the faith, as ye have been taught, abounding therein with thanksgiving. [8] Beware lest any man spoil you through philosophy and vain deceit, after the tradition of men, after the rudiments of the world, and not after Christ."

We received Christ by faith and so we walk in Him by faith.

We're rooted and built up in Him by same faith.

We don't contradict this with the philosophies, vain deceit, and traditions of fallen men.

Romans 1:16 says "For I am not ashamed of the gospel of Christ: for it is the power of God unto salvation to every one that believeth; to the Jew first, and also to the Greek. [17] For therein is the righteousness of God revealed from faith to faith: as it is written, The just shall live by faith."

Righteousness is from faith to faith in the Gospel of Christ and not from faith to logical philosophies.

Take Not Your Holy Spirit From Me

People use King David's prayer in Psalm 51 when he killed a man and took his wife, to teach that God can take His Spirit from a believer in Christ when he commits sins.

Thus, Psalm 51:9 "Hide thy face from my sins, and blot out all mine iniquities. [10] Create in me a clean heart, O God; and renew a right spirit within me. [11] Cast me not away from thy presence; and take not thy holy spirit from me. [12] Restore unto me the joy of thy salvation; and uphold me with thy free spirit."

However, the King was rather longing for the experience of our dispensation of salvation in Christ, when God has blotted out all our iniquities past, present and future, and would not remember them anymore.

Thus, Colossians 2:13 "And you, being dead in your sins and the uncircumcision of your flesh, hath he quickened together with him, having forgiven you all trespasses; [14] Blotting out the handwriting of ordinances that was against us, which was contrary to us, and took it out of the way, nailing it to his cross;"

And also Hebrews 8:12 "For I will be merciful to their unrighteousness, and their sins and their iniquities will I remember no more. [13] In that he saith, A new covenant, he hath made the first old. Now that which decayeth and waxeth old is ready to vanish away."

The Holy Spirit Himself inspired the Prophets to write that a time was coming, which we're now in, when believers' iniquities and unrighteousness would be remembered no more by Him and the Godhead, thus, Hebrews 10:15 "Whereof the Holy Ghost also is a witness to us: for after that he had said before, [16] This is the covenant that I will make with them after those days, saith the Lord, I will put my laws into their hearts, and in their minds will I write them; [17] And their sins and iniquities will I remember no more."

THE DOCTRINE OF POWER; RIGHTLY DIVIDING THE SUPERNATURAL

The Holy Spirit has said it and is fulfilled it now in Christ!

King David was yearning for our days when no believer would be cast out of God's presence but are asked to come boldly, as in Hebrews 4:16 "Let us therefore come boldly unto the throne of grace, that we may obtain mercy, and find grace to help in time of need."

And also, Hebrews 10:19 "Having therefore, brethren, boldness to enter into the holiest by the blood of Jesus, [20] By a new and living way, which he hath consecrated for us, through the veil, that is to say, his flesh; [21] And having an high priest over the house of God; [22] Let us draw near with a true heart in full assurance of faith, having our hearts sprinkled from an evil conscience, and our bodies washed with pure water."

Lastly, King David was afraid that God would take the kingship anointing from him to another, as He took it from Saul to him.

This is because in that time, the kingship anointing (the Holy Spirit then) would only be with the chosen king so would leave the rejected king.

It's not so in God's redemptive plan so don't use it in teaching the Spirit of salvation and redemption in Christ.

You Must Be Born Again

You can be born again based on the Gospel of the death, burial, and resurrection of Jesus Christ that has been revealed in this book.

If you have not yet accepted Christ as your Lord and personal Savior, kindly say this prayer:

Lord God, I acknowledge that I am a sinner. I believe you gave your Son Jesus Christ to be made sin for me on the cross of Calvary so that I may become the righteousness of God in Him by faith. I accept Christ Jesus as my Lord and personal Saviour; I believe He died for me on the cross and was raised on the third day for my justification, therefore I will never perish, in the name of the Lord Jesus Christ, Amen!

Congratulations! You are a new creation in Christ Jesus.

THE DOCTRINE OF POWER; RIGHTLY DIVIDING THE SUPERNATURAL

ABOUT THE AUTHOR

Selasi Evans Noamesi is an anointed man of God who operates in the dynamics of God's power, in healing, miracles and the prophetic. He is a dynamic teacher of the Word of God, bringing fresh insights and revelations from the heart of God in the Bible, through the lens of the Cross of Christ, to the Body of Christ. He is the founder of the Eternal Assembly of Christ, a ministry currently in Ghana, West Africa.

He is a prolific writer who has PhD in Theology.